Catholic for a Reason IV

From the beginning of creation, "God made them male and female." "For this reason a man shall leave his father and mother and be joined to his wife, and the two shall become one."

Mark 10:6

Catholic for a Reason IV
Scripture and the Mystery
of Marriage and Family Life

EDITED BY
SCOTT HAHN, PhD, AND REGIS J. FLAHERTY

EMMAUS
ROAD
PUBLISHING

Steubenville, Ohio
A Division of Catholics United for the Faith

WITH A FOREWORD BY MOST REV. DANIEL CONLON

Emmaus Road Publishing
827 North Fourth Street
Steubenville, OH 43952

© 2007 by Emmaus Road Publishing
All rights reserved. Published 2007
Printed in the United States of America
11 10 09 08 07   1 2 3 4 5   .

Library of Congress Control Number: 2007901734
ISBN: 978-1-931018-44-9

Cover design by
Kinsey Advertising, Inc.
and Beth Hart

Editorial assistance by
Mariann Hughes

CONTENTS

Foreword

The nursery rhyme concludes that Humpty Dumpty couldn't be put together again. Some people today think that marriage faces the same situation. As they see it, no-fault divorce, serial marriages, long-term cohabitation, the "normality" of single-parent and blended families, same-sex unions, prenuptial agreements, contraception as a presumption, and promiscuous sex before and even during marriage have smashed traditional marriage beyond repair. Even some proponents of traditional marriage are ready to throw in the towel.

Fortunately, many people are willing to keep up the good fight—and believe it is winnable, indeed, must be won. Among them are the contributors to *Catholic for a Reason IV: Scripture and the Mystery of Marriage and Family Life.*

The volume is replete with solid Catholic theology and idealism. Curtis and Stacy Mitch express them poignantly in the third article: "Grace is poured out in superabundance to enrich married life and to make married couples living icons of God's unfailing love for the world." That marriage, specifically a permanent union between a man and a woman who are open to children, is an irrevocable part of God's design for His human children and an essential cell of human society is proclaimed unabashedly.

While reaffirming the natural law, the authors also sketch out the unique qualities of Christian, sacramental marriage. They cite frequently the teachings of the Second Vatican Council and recent popes, especially John Paul II. I found Regis and Libbie Flaherty's analysis of the revolutionary attitudes toward marriage among early Christians especially insightful. "This way of life was possible only because it was part of the Christian vocation. It was a free response to the call to love God and neighbor." What an excellent, and promising, basis for matrimonial catechesis in today's Church and world.

Scripture and the Mystery of Marriage and Family Life is not all theology, however. In fact, it is filled with the concrete experiences of married couples who strive to live out their vocation day by day with God's help. Many of their examples of marriage and family life are touching—and very real.

I am blessed to know some of the authors personally. I have even been invited into their homes. Their commitment to marriage and their witness to its joys and struggles are authentic. They are true believers, and out of the gift of their own love they desire to help other married couples and parents discover, or rediscover, the joys of marriage and family life, as God intended it.

As the Mitches put it, "Christians believe that Jesus Christ redeemed mankind, and, in the process, redeemed the covenant of marriage. The Lord came among us to pull marriage from the wreckage of human sin and restore its magnificence once again." The Lord is still at it. Humpty Dumpty can—and must—be put together again.

† Most Reverend R. Daniel Conlon
Bishop of Steubenville

Abbreviations

1 Pet.	1 Peter
2 Pet.	2 Peter
1 Jn.	1 John
2 Jn.	2 John
3 Jn.	3 John
Jude	Jude
Rev.	Revelation (Apocalypse)

DOCUMENTS OF VATICAN II

SC   Constitution on the Sacred Liturgy
(*Sacrosanctum Concilium*), December 4, 1963

LG   Dogmatic Constitution on the Church
(*Lumen Gentium*), November 21, 1964

GS   Pastoral Constitution on the Church in the
Modern World (*Gaudium et Spes*), December 7, 1965

OTHER ABBREVIATIONS

FC   Pope John Paul II, Apostolic Exhortation
On the Role of the Christian Family in the Modern World
Familiaris Consortio (November 22, 1981)

HV   Pope Paul VI, Encyclical On Human Life
Humanae Vitae (June 25, 1968)

LXX   The Greek Septuagint

CHAPTER I

The World
as Wedding

SCOTT HAHN

The first wedding I ever attended was my own. Nothing previous in life had quite prepared me for that moment—or for the several months leading up to the vows. Sure, there were probing heart-to-heart talks with my future in-laws, and the prep-and-pep talks from friends in the clergy. Kimberly and I were both, after all, preparing for careers in the Presbyterian church, so we were always surrounded by eager counselors.

But, for me at least, the mad dash to matrimony was a completely new experience. No one had told me what to expect, and I had never seen it for myself. There were budgets to be drawn up, gowns to be measured, guest lists to be compiled, invitations to be sent, a hall to be booked, tuxes to be rented, and bridesmaids and groomsmen to be choreographed.

All this filled to overflowing two lives that had already seemed over-full. At the time of our engagement, we were serious students in challenging undergraduate programs, both preparing for graduate school and both very active in youth ministry. Who had time for wedding planning?

But, like the tides and the seasons, wedding plans are inexorable things, and we've all got to do what we've all got to do. So I let myself be directed by Kimberly, who had observed a few weddings during her teen years, and I abandoned myself to task after task. In those final weeks, whenever I wasn't sleeping, I was making phone calls, running errands, licking stamps, having something measured, or stating my color preference.

Still, I never got to the end of the to-do list. The day arrived, and I found myself standing at the front of the church, beside my best man, my mind still turning over a thousand details and loose ends.

That's when the processional music changed, and that's when I had the vision.

It wasn't quite a new heaven and a new earth, but it might as well have been. It was a new Kimberly. Or, rather, it was Kimberly as I had never seen her before. Her dress was white and seemingly radiant in the sunny church of a late-summer afternoon. But that's not what astonished me. It was her face, now beneath a veil. In all those months of preparation and decisions, I had never once seen even a photograph of her veil and gown; nor had I given them a thought. Yet now this vision struck me as something new and beautiful and deeply mysterious—something holy.

I was literally taken aback. I remember that I actually staggered.

For me it seemed that that very moment contained all of my life, all of history, and all of creation. And, in a sense, it did. The Bible tells us so.

A Garden-Variety Love Story

I am not the first reader to note that the Bible is a book that tells a love story—the story of God's love for humankind. As if to emphasize the point, the Church arranged the Scriptures so that the biblical canon begins and ends with a wedding. In Genesis, the high point of the creation narrative is God's fashioning of man and woman, Adam and Eve, the primal two who become one flesh (Gen. 2:23–24). In John's apocalypse, Revelation, the culmination is at the very end, in the seer's vision of heaven, which his angel guide describes as "the marriage supper of the Lamb" (Rev. 19:9)—the celebration of the communion of Christ and His Church.

In between those two events, a love story unfolds. But the drama depends so much upon that opening scene in Genesis that we should pause there for a moment and consider what took place.

It is a familiar sequence of events. God created Adam and gave him dominion over the garden of Eden. Genesis describes man's dominion in terms that, elsewhere in the Scriptures, are used to describe priestly duties. God places man in the garden "to till it and keep it" (Gen. 2:15); the Hebrew verbs rendered "till" and "keep" ('abodah and shamar) appear together elsewhere in the Pentateuch only to describe the priestly ministry of the Levites (see Num. 3:7–8, 8:26, 18:5–6). The Levites were to "serve" and "guard" the sanctuary, keeping it safe and pure from profanation. Adam was to do the same for the garden. Thus, God gave Adam all the world for his possession, and He charged him to preside over it all, not just with kingly dominion, but with priestly holiness.

Adam had dominion over creation. His possessions, however, were not enough to satisfy his human nature. God had made Adam to find completion outside himself and apart from his worldly goods: "It is not good that the man should be alone; I will make him a helper fit for him" (Gen. 2:18). Then God formed Eve from one of Adam's ribs, and He made her so well that Adam exclaimed, "This at last is bone of my bones and flesh of my flesh" (Gen. 2:23). Adam's vocation was to love, as God loves.

Yet his bliss was short-lived; for we immediately read the story of the deadly serpent, his empty promises, and Adam and Eve's violation of the only limit God had placed on their dominion: "Of the tree of the knowledge of good and evil you shall not eat, for in the day that you eat of it you shall die" (Gen. 2:17).

We may see this not only as disobedience, but as fear and neglect as well. It was Adam's job, after all, to protect the garden sanctuary and keep it from profanation. It was his duty to protect

his bride. Yet, he failed by allowing the serpent to enter their home
and begin his fearsome dialogue of temptation.

Adam's sin was pride; he disobeyed God and placed his own
safety before his bride's. He failed to lay down his life to save
hers. His was a failure of love, and so he proved incapable of living the divine life that God had intended to share with humanity.
Moreover, Adam left his human family a legacy of dysfunction
that cascaded down the generations—and the sign of this dysfunction, beginning in Genesis itself, is marital disarray. Sin expresses
itself as polygamy (Gen. 4:19–24), incest (Gen. 19:31–38), and
sodomy (Gen. 19:4–11). Eventually, the greatest sin of Israel's
greatest king, David, would begin with adultery (2 Sam. 11:1–13).
Solomon's polygamy would lead him to idolatry (1 Kings 11:1–9),
as Abraham's practice of concubinage had led to horrific strife
(Gen. 16:1–15; 21:8–21).

Still, though the primal catastrophe surely wounded nature,
marriage remained a great good. And it remained God's favorite
metaphor for His love for humankind. He cast His relationship
with man in terms of covenant—a sacred bond of kinship sealed
by a solemn oath. In the ancient world, covenant was the bond
that formed families. Marriage was perhaps the most common
form of covenant.

Covenant or Contract?

It is important for us to get this right. But, in order to do so,
we have to move beyond certain modern assumptions and retrieve
the sense of covenant as it was lived in biblical cultures—and not
only in the Hebrew and Christian religious cultures, but also in
the Gentile and pagan societies of the ancient world. For covenant
was the foundation of these societies. It gave individual persons
their sense of kinship, their sense of relationship, their sense of
belonging—to a family, a tribe, and a nation. The covenant oath
was the foundation of family, national, and religious life.

In today's legal usage, the words contract and covenant are
almost interchangeable. But that was not true in the ancient
world. Every covenant was based upon a contractual agreement,

but a covenant differed from a contract in many ways.[1] I'd like to mention just a few.

In contracts, the terms are negotiable; in covenants, they are not. God sets the terms of the covenant. The people may freely choose to accept or reject those terms, but rejecting the terms means the loss of any share in the covenant blessings.

Contracts are based upon the parties making promises; while covenants are only entered through the solemn swearing of an oath (*sacramentum* in Latin).

Contracts are normally based on profit; covenants are based on love. The former speaks to self-interest, while the latter calls us to self-sacrifice.

Contracts exchange goods and services; covenants exchange persons.

Contracts are legal devices; they are conditional, and they can be broken. A covenant is more of a social organism; it is unconditional and ongoing. Even when it is violated, it is not thereby dissolved.

Contracts are limited in scope; covenants affect many (if not all) areas of life.

Contracts are limited in duration; covenants last for life, even extending to future generations.

We could list many other differences between contracts and covenants, but these will suffice. For we can see in these differences that every covenant includes a contractual element, but also that the covenant far surpasses the mere contract and establishes a much different kind of relationship.

The differences show us that God's covenantal relationship with humankind is non-negotiable, but freely accepted; that it is

---

[1] On the differences between covenants and contracts in Scripture, particularly with reference to marriage, see Scott Hahn, *Swear to God: The Promise and Power of the Sacraments* (New York: Doubleday, 2004); John Grabowski, *Sex and Virtue: An Introduction to Sexual Ethics* (Washington, DC: Catholic University of America Press, 2003), 32–38; Gordon P. Hugenberger, *Marriage as a Covenant: A Study of Biblical Law and Ethics* (Leiden: Brill 1995), 185–279; Paul F. Palmer, S.J., "Christian Marriage: Covenant or Contract?" *Theological Studies* 33 (1972), 617–665; G. M. Tucker, "Covenant Forms and Contracts Forms," *Vetus Testamentum* 15 (1965), 487–503.

based on love; that it involves a sharing of our very lives—and His very life; that it is unlimited in scope. And that it is forever. In all of this, the divine covenant is very much like a marriage.

The Prophet Motive

When God spoke through the prophets, He taught Israel always to hope and strive for the renewal of His covenant. And, again, He portrayed the covenant as a marriage. He spoke of Himself, or His Messiah, coming as a bridegroom to take His people as His bride (see Hos. 2:16–24; Jer. 2:2; Is. 54:4–8).

Human marriage, then, was for Israel an earthly image of God's eternal love. Jon Levenson of Harvard, a contemporary Jewish scholar, explains that the Hebrew Scriptures are incomprehensible apart from this nuptial key:

> What happened on the mountain in the ancient days was the consummation of a romance, a marriage in which YHWH was the groom and Israel . . . was the bride. Thus, a book like Deuteronomy, which is saturated with the idiom of the covenant, sees in the selection of Israel to be YHWH's treasured possession, the fruit of a passionate affair (Deut. 7:6–8).[2]

Some people wrongly caricature Israelite religion as "legalistic," simply because of its emphasis on the Law of the covenant. But Levenson makes clear: "It is not a question of law or love, but law conceived in love, love expressed in law. The two are a unity."[3]

And the joy is not only for Israel. All creation is caught up in the celebration of this "wedding" of heaven and earth. Through the prophet Hosea, God promises: "I will make for you a covenant on that day with the beasts of the field, the birds of the air, and the creeping things of the ground; and I will abolish the bow, the sword, and war from the land; and I will make you lie down in safety. And I will betroth you to me for ever; I will betroth you to me in righteousness and in justice, in steadfast

---

[2] Jon Levenson, *Sinai and Zion: An Entry into the Jewish Bible* (San Francisco: Harper-Collins, 1985), 76.

[3] Levenson, *Sinai and Zion*, 77.

love, and in mercy. I will betroth you to me in faithfulness; and you shall know the LORD" (2:18–20). Levenson concludes: "In the last stanza of Hosea's prophecy (vs. 23–25), all creation joins in the wedding ceremony. Sky responds to earth, and earth responds by bringing forth her bounty. . . . The entire universe takes part in the sacred remarriage of YHWH and Israel."[4]

Rabbi Michael Fishbane traces the influence of marital imagery from Hosea to Jeremiah (see Jer. 2:2, 3:1). But, above all, he writes: "The topic of covenantal love between God and Israel came to celebrated expression in the classical rabbinic interpretations of the Song of Songs."[5] Which tradition, a Christian might add, is found in the continuation of the Church's saints and scholars, from Origen and Gregory of Nyssa through Bernard of Clairvaux and Thomas Aquinas to Jacques Maritain and Pope John Paul II.

The prophets heralded a new and everlasting covenant, which would be a renewal of the original covenant between God and Adam, God and humankind, God and all creation. It would, in fact, be so all-encompassing as to be a "new creation." The imagery of the prophets, which was employed in turn by Jesus Christ, was the imagery of betrothal and marriage. Thus, when Jesus came, He called Himself the "bridegroom" and those who were united to Him in baptism were called "espoused" (see Jn. 3:29; Mk. 2:19; Mt. 22:1–14, 25:1–13; 1 Cor. 6:15–17; 2 Cor. 11:2; see also CCC 796).

Unveiled Intentions

Interestingly, it is Jesus who gave us the first explicitly marital interpretation of Genesis. The word "marriage," after all, had not appeared in the story of Adam and Eve. Yet, we know the story is about marriage because Jesus said it was (see Mk. 10:2–16). Jesus said that the Genesis story reflects God's will "from the beginning of creation" and that "what God has joined together, no human being must separate."

---

[4] Ibid, 79.
[5] Michael Fishbane, *JPS Bible Commentary: Haftarot* (Philadelphia: Jewish Publication Society, 2002), 555–556.

Further along in the New Testament, Saint Paul provides a profound mystical commentary. In his Letter to the Ephesians, he quotes the Genesis text and explains that this marriage covenant in the Garden is a reference to the covenant between "Christ and the Church" (see Eph. 5:21–33). In using this unquestionable allusion to Adam and Eve becoming one flesh, Paul seems also to be shedding light on Adam's task and failure. He helps us see that Adam did not "give himself up" for his bride as he should have, and he helps us see that Christ does indeed "give Himself up" for His bride, the Church. Where the first Adam had failed, with dire consequences, the new Adam succeeded, with saving power.

Note that Paul does not cancel out the literal meaning of the Genesis text, nor does he say it is not truly about husbands and wives. In fact, he gives a beautiful teaching on the love that husbands and wives share. But he is telling us that marriage is also a symbol of a far greater mystery—the love that Christ has for His bride, the Church, the love that God has for His people.

This mystery receives its most powerful expression in the last book of the Bible, the Revelation of Saint John, otherwise known as the Apocalypse—from the Greek word *apokalypsis*, which literally means "unveiling." Like the story of Adam and Eve, the Apocalypse evokes images that are both nuptial and priestly, for veils were then, as now, a standard part of a bride's wardrobe. The bride's "unveiling"—apokalypsis—was the culmination of the Jews' traditional weeklong wedding feast. Indeed, apokalypsis became associated with the first moment of marital intimacy and bodily communion, the physical consummation of the nuptial covenant.[6]

---

[6] See Karel van der Toorn, "The Significance of the Veil in the Ancient Near East," in David Noel Freedman et al. (eds.), *Pomegranates and Golden Bells: Studies in Biblical, Jewish, and Near Eastern Ritual, Law and Literature* (Winona Lake, IN: Eisenbrauns, 1995), 327–338. After noting how "the principal ceremony in which the veil played a role is the wedding" (p. 330), van der Toorn observes: "While the importance of the bridal veil in the wedding ceremonial is generally acknowledged, it has not sufficiently been noted that the veil occurs in a dual capacity. Many studies dwell only on the veil as a symbol of chastity or virginity . . . [but] the bride came to the groom veiled . . . so that he might unveil her in privacy." He cites Jacob's attempt to marry Rachel (after *seven* years of work and a *seven*-day wedding): "The substitution of Leah for Rachel could only be successful

Like a bride, God's sanctuary was veiled, to be unveiled only with the consummation of the New Covenant (see Mk. 15:38). The holy of holies in Jerusalem's temple was a four-square sanctuary, overlaid with gold (1 Kg. 6:19–20), shielded from sight by a floor-to-ceiling veil, a curtain embroidered with animal and floral decorations. Thus, nature itself appeared as a "veil" of an even greater reality. Yet that veil was torn, literally and symbolically, when Christ's body was torn in His act of self-giving love on the Cross. Because of His self-offering, "we have confidence to enter the sanctuary by the blood of Jesus, by the new and living way which he opened for us through the veil, that is, through his flesh" (Heb. 10:19–20).

---

if it was a custom for the bride to be veiled when entering the premises where the wedding was celebrated" (p. 331; cf. Gen. 29:18–30). He adds: "The unveiling there…signals readiness to undress as a prelude to sexual intercourse" (p. 338). Also see R. de Vaux, *Ancient Israel: Its Life and Institutions* (New York: McGraw-Hill, 1961), 33–34: "she wore a veil (Ct 4:1, 3; 6:7), which she took off only in the bridal chamber." See A. Bertholet, *A History of Hebrew Civilization* (New York: Brentanos, 1926), p. 189, n. 189, who explains how the Hebrew word "to know" (*yada'*) came to denote sexual intercourse, since it was at the moment of marital consummation that the bridegroom actually saw his bride (now unveiled) for the first time; cf. David Mace, *Hebrew Marriage: A Sociological Study* (London: Epworth, 1953), 182. See the word-study of *apokalypsis* (and related terms) by Albrecht Oepke in G. Kittel (ed.), *Theological Dictionary of the New Testament* III (Grand Rapids, MI: Eerdmans, 1979), 556–571. "Of the many meanings, the only one that has theological significance is that of 'head-covering' or 'veil'" (p. 558); yet he cites a number of cultic texts where a "veil" has sacred uses: "'Cover' e.g., for the tent of revelation, Ex. 27:16, also before the Holy of Holies, Ex. 40:5," and then notes: "In the OT it acquires a sacral sense not only as used anatomically in sacrificial regulations (Ex. 29:22 etc.) but also in the command that Moses should place the ark within the Holy of Holies and hide it from sight behind the curtain (Ex. 26:34)." In sum, not only Jewish brides, but Israel's holiest places and persons, were typically veiled. Oepke cites the case of Susanna (p. 562), "a woman of great refinement and beautiful in appearance . . . the wicked men commanded to unveil (*apokalypsthenai*) her face, for she was veiled" (LXX Dan. 13:31–32; cf. Lev. 18:6–19, where *apokalypseis* occurs seventeen times all within the context of Israel's sexual and cultic purity laws). On the meaning (and nuptial overtones) of *apokalypsis* in the Book of Revelation, see D. A. McIlraith, *The Reciprocal Love Between Christ and the Church in the Apocalypse* (Rome: Pontifical Gregorian University, 1989), 94–109; 123–147; 170–204. Also see G. W. Buchanan, *The Book of Revelation* (Lewiston, NY: Edwin Mellen Press, 1993), 33: "The word translated 'revelation' can mean something uncovered, such as a revealed woman is one who has no clothing. . . . The term rendered 'naked' or 'unclothed' was also used to tell of a message Daniel received, informing him of the events that were to happen in the future" (cf. LXX Dan. 10:1). Also see M. Smith, "On the History of *Apokalypto* and *Apokalypsis*" in *Studies in the Cult of Yahweh II: New Testament and Early Christianity* (Leiden: Brill, 1996), 194–205.

That which is veiled is holy, to be unveiled only in covenant love. What the Apocalypse "unveils" is history's final consummation, the marriage of Christ to His bride, the Church (see Rev. 19:9, 21:9, 22:17). She is "the holy city, New Jerusalem, coming down out of heaven from God, prepared as a bride adorned for her husband" (Rev. 21:2). Like the holy of holies, Christ's bride is four-square and resplendent with pure gold (Rev. 21:16–18).

By "unveiling" the Church, our priestly Bridegroom reveals the gift of His love to His bride—the New Jerusalem—in the "glory and beauty" of the Spirit (see Ex. 28:2). And what else? The New Creation—"a new heaven and a new earth" (Rev. 21:1).

It is a reprise of the opening chapters of Genesis. The third-century scholar Origen held that John's Apocalypse was the interpretive key to John's Gospel. Indeed, many puzzling aspects of the wedding feast at Cana seem to clear up when we understand that John is describing a new Genesis, a new creation, an eschatological "wedding feast" of the Lamb of God.[7]

In the first covenant, we saw the marriage union of a man and a woman, Adam and Eve (see Gen. 2:23–24). In the new covenant, we see a new man and a new woman present at a wedding feast. True, Mary is Jesus' mother, not His bride. But in order to understand the supernatural depths of biblical symbolism that John intends here, we need to set aside our "natural" ways of reading. As the "woman," Mary becomes the locus of a host of biblical symbols and expectations. She is simultaneously a daughter of Israel, the mother of the new people of God, and the bride of God.

Notice who is not mentioned in John's account—the couple being married. Isn't it odd that a wedding feast would be described, but not the bride and groom? Saint Augustine commented: "What marvel, if He went to that house to a marriage,

---

[7] On the correlation of John and Revelation, see the remarkable study by Warren Austin Gage, "St John's Vision of the Heavenly City" (PhD Dissertation, University of Dallas; Ann Arbor, MI: UMI, 2001).

Who came into this world of a marriage. For here He has His spouse whom He redeemed with His own blood, to whom He united Himself in the womb of the Virgin. For the Word is the Bridegroom, and human flesh the bride, and both together are one Son of God and Son of Man."[8]

At Cana, Jesus appears as a new Adam, the firstborn of a new creation. What John implies is made clear elsewhere in the New Testament. Paul calls Jesus a "type" of Adam (see Rom. 5:14) and the new or last Adam (see 1 Cor. 15:21–22, 45–49). At Cana, Mary is the New Eve, the bride of the New Adam, the mother of the new creation.

At Cana comes the changing of water into wine—a transubstantiation that foreshadows Jesus' New Covenant meal: the Eucharist, the bodily consummation of the covenant between God and His Church.[9] It is in the Eucharist that Jesus gives us His Body as food (Jn. 6:26–58), and we, God's children, "share in flesh and blood" (Heb. 2:14). It is in the Eucharist that Jesus draws all humanity to the marriage supper of the Lamb. It is in the Eucharist that Christ can look upon the Church as Adam looked upon Eve and say, "This at last is bone of my bones and flesh of my flesh" (Gen. 2:23).

In the Eucharist, we are made members of the wedding, each of us seated at the head table of the "marriage feast" that Jesus called "my banquet" in His parables. In the Eucharist, we enter into the depths of the communion of love that God intends for each person. In baptism, each of us was "betrothed to Christ" (2 Cor. 11:2). Every Eucharist is our nuptial feast. "Every celebration," Augustine said, "is a celebration of marriage—the Church's nuptials are celebrated. The King's Son

---

[8] Saint Augustine, *Commentary on John*, Tractate viiii, c. 4, quoted in the *Catena Aurea* of Saint Thomas Aquinas.

[9] The Fathers did not miss the symbolism of Jesus performing His first miracle at a wedding, in a miracle that foreshadowed the Eucharist. Cyril of Jerusalem wrote: "Christ has changed water into wine, which is akin to blood, at Cana of Galilee. Invited to the visible wedding, he accomplished this first miracle. . . . [Now] he has given to the children of the bridal chamber the joy of his body and blood." Quoted in Jean Danielou, *The Bible and the Liturgy* (Notre Dame, IN: Notre Dame University Press, 1956), 220.

is about to marry a wife and . . . the guests frequenting the marriage are themselves the Bride. . . . For all the Church is Christ's Bride."[10]

What Is Veiled Is Holy

It is true of the temple, and it is true of the bride. The connection is eminently clear in Jesus' mother tongue. The Hebrew word for holiness is *kiddushin*, which is also the word used for the Jewish wedding ceremony and for the state of matrimony.[11]

When I first saw Kimberly on our wedding day, her beauty, even veiled, nearly knocked me off my feet. It was something mysterious, so much more than I could have expected. That wedding was a revelation to me. Little did I know that it was only a beginning, a genesis, a new creation, a new covenant.

> Then came one of the seven angels . . . saying, "Come, I will show you the Bride, the wife of the Lamb." And in the Spirit he carried me away to a great, high mountain, and showed me the holy city Jerusalem coming down out of heaven from God, having the glory of God, its radiance like a most rare jewel, like a jasper, clear as crystal. (Rev. 21:9–11)

Discussion Questions

1. What are the differences between a covenant and a contract?
2. What is "unveiled" in the Book of Revelation? What does this reality mean for the Church now and at the culmination of time?
3. How does Christ's miracle at the wedding at Cana foreshadow the Eucharist? How is the Eucharist a "marriage feast"?

---

[10] Quoted in Claude Chavasse, *The Bride of Christ* (London: Faber and Faber, 1939), 147.

[11] See Rabbi Maurice Lamm, *The Jewish Way in Love and Marriage* (San Francisco: Harper & Row, 1980), 208: "*The veil is symbolic of her new unapproachability to others, not only sexually but as* hekdesh, *a sanctified object in the temple.* The sacred objects of the tabernacle were 'veiled' before being taken up to be carried by the Levites. The betrothal ceremony is likened, in a legal sense, to those sanctified objects of the temple. This is the significance of the term *kiddushin*: the groom, in marriage, sets the bride aside as *hekdesh*."

Dr. Scott Hahn is founder, president, and chairman of the Board of The St. Paul Center for Biblical Theology. He is professor of theology at Franciscan University of Steubenville, and was recently appointed to the Pope Benedict XVI Chair of Biblical Theology at St. Vincent Seminary (Latrobe, Pa.). He is also author or editor of more than 20 books, including Scripture Matters *(Emmaus Road Publishing, 2003) and* Understanding "Our Father": Biblical Reflections on the Lord's Prayer *(Emmaus Road Publishing, 2002). He has more than one million books and tapes in print worldwide.*

CHAPTER II

The World after the Wedding

KIMBERLY HAHN

"The World as a Wedding" provides us a breathtaking view of the magnificence of the wedding nuptials of Christ and His Bride, the Church, joining Heaven and earth. This lofty image isn't just the attractive topping on the wedding cake—it's the substance of the Sacrament itself. Our understanding of God's marital love and fidelity to His beloved people provides the backdrop for each of our individual marriages; our individual marriages provide the backdrop for a witness to the world of the relationship between Christ and His Church. So, how do we bring this aerial view into pinpoint focus on our marriage?

Prepare More for Marriage than for Wedding

Throughout our days of engagement, my mom and dad would remind Scott and me to prepare more for marriage than for our wedding day. Why? As significant a feast day as our wedding day would be, we needed to prepare more for our life together.

This wisdom was driven home by a comment from a friend, the only child of a well-to-do couple, who had not followed this advice. The couple's approach to the wedding had been a spareno-expense extravaganza, though the financial circumstances of her beloved were meager at best. Following a bridal shower for me, she spoke of sadness that clearly colored her outlook on life: "I awoke two days after our wedding to the realization that I'm going to clean toilets for the rest of my life!"

Though Scott and I are continually grateful for each other, we don't necessarily rise in the morning with ecstatic honeymoon-type utterances of "I love you with all of my heart!" or "I can't believe I'm married to you!" Rather, we rise to the tasks of the day, demonstrating our love and faithfulness as we do the ordinary things that need to be done.

Likewise, the birth of a child brings great joy and wonderment; yet, life is not lived in the thrill of the birth, no matter how much we love this child. We don't usually greet our children at breakfast saying, "I am your mother!" "You're my beloved daughter!" or "I'm so grateful for a son like you!" It would be great if we verbalized our feelings more often, but ordinary life, in general, is not lived that way.

There's a reason why there is more "ordinary" time in a liturgical year than special days. More of life is lived in the ordinary, while the extraordinary enlarges our understanding of the ordinary.

Ordinary time—what does that mean? It is the normal everyday type of religious day (for all days are religious though all days are not meant for fasting or feasting). Ordinary time marks the day in, day out challenge of living one more day for the Lord, faithful to the mundane tasks. In ordinary time we plod along, doing the next thing that needs to be done, knowing that even that nondescript day is part of our long obedience in the same direction.

Menial Work is Not Meaningless Work

Typical homemaking tasks don't usually get me down. Sure, doing the same chores week after week can get tedious, but I was trained by my mother to see the spiritual side of things—it's possible to rise above the mundane to see the big picture.

Then, one day, I stopped in my tracks with a basket full of clothes, mid-way up the stairs. There it was—the same Healthtex

shirt I had laundered for years. Michael had worn it, Gabriel had
worn it (Hannah had not worn it, since it was too boyish), and
Jeremiah had worn it. Now, week after week, I carried it up the
stairs for Joseph, only to have him get it dirty again! I was caught,
for a moment, in the futility of what I was doing. The laundry
basket almost became too heavy to carry. How many times had
I washed this one shirt? All of a sudden I felt snagged on a point
of self-pity—the futility of it all.

I cried out, "God help me! How many times am I going to
wash this shirt? What's the point of all this repetitive work?"

Almost immediately, the Lord brought to mind a simple but
marvelous thought: "Think how many children you have been able
to love, week after week, through this one little shirt." All of a sudden the load felt light, and I easily carried it up the stairs.

I realized, with gratitude, that though the work was repetitive,
the work on my heart and mind was not. The task hadn't changed;
I had. Through the mundane work of a homemaker, God was
fashioning a home in my heart where love could be expressed
in myriad acts of kindness, including laundering the same shirt,
which, by the way, has only recently been retired from active duty
since David has outgrown it!

Though I may be sweeping the same floor, wiping the same
dishes, making the same bed, and washing the same clothes,
something is different—I am. Little by little, God is giving me
more of a servant heart as I relinquish my will to His, as I allow
the ordinary tasks of a typical day to reflect the extraordinary
love He has for my loved ones through me.

What in the World Are We Doing?

We were made by God, for God. He created each one of us
for a purpose. All that we have is a gift from Him, and He calls
us to give ourselves back to Him as a gift. For those of us who are
married, we have been called to be a living reflection of Him to
our spouse, our children, and to those touched by our family.

Before I was a Catholic, while in Joliet, Illinois, I often overheard conversations between college students that went like this:

"Do you have a vocation?"

"No, I'm getting married."

I asked my husband Scott, "Is that a Catholic answer?"

"No," he quickly rejoined. "Marriage *is* a vocation."

Marriage, in fact, is our path to holiness—as long as we discern Him in the middle of the muddle! We have the journey of a lifetime ahead of us, to grow in faith with our spouse so that we will enjoy our Lord together forever. But how do we receive and maintain our sense of mission? How do we live our lives as lay people so that we fulfill this vision?

Priority *loving* leads us to priority *living*.

Before we can love our spouse or children properly, we need to cultivate our love for God. He must be our deepest love from whom we draw the strength and the grace to love all others well. We may have all kinds of natural virtues, good habits, and a kind nature, but we will not raise a godly family without the grace of God.

Individual prayer is not a luxury we try to fit into our packed schedule; it's a necessity. Whether or not prayer can occur before little ones' demands must be addressed—how do they seem to sense I am trying to pray alone first thing in the morning?—we need to drink from the well of God's presence in order to refresh others. Family prayer helps but it cannot substitute for our own one-on-one time with our Heavenly Father.

Loving God means resting in His presence (at home in prayer, before the Blessed Sacrament in adoration, or at Mass). We share the concerns on our hearts and we regain His peace-filled perspective. When we renew our consecration for the day, our works, joys, and sufferings of that day become an extension of our prayer. We become heavenly-minded so that we can be earthly good.

God is the One who teaches us how to love all others, including ourselves. He leads us to love ourselves as He loves us, to accept His acceptance of us. He lavishes His grace and forgiveness on us, and in response, we are able to extend grace and forgiveness to our spouse and children. He inspires gratitude for all He has given us, including the gift of our spouse and children.

The Core Relationship of the Family: Marriage

Recently, I referred to one of my children as "my sweet love," to which another child responded, "I thought *I* was your sweet love. Am I your sweetest love?"

"All of you children are my sweet loves," I answered. "But Daddy is my sweetest love." My comment elicited groans along with big smiles.

Priority loving in the family means loving your spouse first, your children second. The love of husband and wife is the wellspring of love for the entire family. Though our children's needs seem greater and more immediate, we must be careful not to allow their needs to consume the time and energy needed for our spouse. Besides, the greatest need of our children is to experience the love of their parents for each other. Often when my husband and I embrace, our young children try to wedge between us—not to break us apart but to feel the squeeze of love.

In marriage, we have opportunities to model for our children the kind of compassionate care and sacrificial service we long for them to imitate. Dying to ourselves sounds more dramatic than denying ourselves in small ways each day. For instance, it sounds grand and noble for a man to lay down his life for his wife. However, usually, marriage involves other tasks: laying down a fork when the food is hot to change a diaper, laying down the TV remote to wash the pots, laying down a good book to take out the trash, or not lying down in order to help with the carpool. Much smaller sacrifices though they are, they are still challenging enough to our residual selfishness. Patiently God guides us to give more and more of ourselves so that we can receive more and more of Him. After all, Jesus came to serve rather than be served, and we are to imitate Him.

Even when we fail, we still can model forgiveness and a sense of a new beginning. We aren't saints yet, but we want to be saints. And we want them to join us on this path of holiness.

Holiness is not an individual marathon, when you are married, trying to do an end run round your spouse. Rather, the path to sanctity is a relay race where we pass the baton back and forth, running alongside each other, urging each other on when it is difficult, assisting whoever may be falling behind. It's not a static state of being, but an ecstatic, fluid process of getting closer to God and thereby getting closer to each other.

Our Home, a Domestic Church

When we parents share our spiritual journey, our children witness not only our individual love for God but also our united love for Him. They are drawn closer to God as they follow our lead. More is caught from us than taught by us, though it's essential that we teach them about the Lord, too. They share in the spirit of generosity of life, the care for any who are sick, the compassion toward those who are suffering, and the sense of celebration for those who are rejoicing. It is in this spirit that the family functions as a domestic church.

One of the great privileges we have within marriage is cooperation with God in the creation of new life. When He enables us to create the body of the child, He blesses the child with a soul. Through Baptism, we enrich the Church with this new child of God, and then we do all we can to share the faith, day in and day out, with this child so that we'll not only enjoy this life together but can anticipate eternity together. Our children also enter into this sharing of the faith as they pray with each other and teach each other. When one of our children was sick, I overheard another son say, "Can you offer up your flu for someone who needs prayer?"

With barely a pause, I watched this sick little one bow his head and offer his feeling sick "for a woman somewhere, God, who is thinking about having an abortion." I brushed away tears at his simple yet remarkable heart for someone he didn't know.

We also love our children in myriad ways throughout the day (and night!)—day after day, week after week. Many of the tasks of married life don't seem very spiritual—fix the car, do the laundry, cook, clean, earn a paycheck, weed the garden, help with homework, etc. Yet every task has a spiritual dimension, provided we do it with great love, as Saint Therese of Lisieux reminds us.

Corporal Works of Mercy in our Homes

We do not have to leave our homes to live the meaning of Jesus' words in Matthew 25:34–40. We "feed the hungry" and "give a drink to the thirsty" by providing nutritional and delicious meals around a table of love. When we welcome them home to a safe harbor from the storms of life, we "welcome the stranger." By caring for their needs for comfortable, modest, and attractive clothing, we "clothe the naked;" by caring for their bodies when they are ill, we "visit the sick." And during those times when growing pains for independence challenge our sanity and our sanctity, whether they are toddlers or teens, it can feel like we "visit the imprisoned."

Saint Paul offers these words of encouragement in Galatians 6:9: "Don't grow weary in well doing." It is easy to care for a dependent, cuddly baby who coos and smiles and stays where you put him. It is more difficult, and more rewarding, to care for other loved ones who, like us, have not yet attained sainthood!

We are often inspired by saints who endured great trials and sufferings for Christ—whippings, beatings, deprivation, and death. Yet these are not the sufferings asked of most of us. Rather, we are asked to give one more cup of water at night to a child we settled an hour earlier, to launder one more outfit after we have already finished cleaning clothes for the week, to go on one more errand on a cold, dark night when we were ready to go to bed, to make one more unexpected visit to the doctor's office at the time we were supposed to leave for a holiday (all the while wondering what new germs we are adding to the mix just being there!). Our sufferings are real and they are valuable, when they are offered in union with the cross.

A Vision of the Invisible

If we can catch the vision for what the vocation of marriage can be, we will embrace all that is challenging. What stalls our progress and what can we do?

Sometimes we fall into the trap of comparison—the ideal of what we want our marriage and family life to be versus the reality of our experience. Though it is fine to have an ideal to shoot for, it can be crushing to feel as if it is unattainable. However, the Lord wants us to have the hope that grace is at work in ways we do not see. The Lord wants us to lift our vision higher, to look beyond the visible to the greater invisible reality of what He is doing in and through our marriage and family life. This spiritual dimension of what is happening is every bit as real as our daily experiences.

When we feel weak, we can recall Jesus' words to Saint Paul: "My grace is sufficient for you, for my power is made perfect in weakness" (2 Cor. 12:9). In other words, you are weak but I (Jesus) am strong and I'll do My will through you.

When we feel inadequate, we remember the example of Our Lady who, when she received the news that she was to be the mother of the Son of God, proclaimed not her abilities but her availability: "Behold, I am the handmaid of the Lord; let it be to me according to thy word" (Lk. 1:38). Our vocation is not based on how gifted we are but on how willing we are to serve.

When we feel anxious, we follow the advice of Saint Paul: "Have no anxiety about anything, but in everything, by prayer and supplication, let your requests be made known unto God and the peace of God which passes all understanding will keep your hearts and your minds in Christ Jesus" (Phil. 4:6, 7). We allow our concerns to bring us to the One who has called us into this marvelous vocation; He will give us His peace.

In his great chapter on love, Saint Paul writes, "Love bears all things, believes all things, hopes all things, endures all things" (1 Cor. 13:7). Our love imitates God's love when we come alongside each other, rejoicing with loved ones when they rejoice, and weeping with them when they weep. Our love imitates God's love when we regain His perspective on our life, especially through the Mass where the grid of reality descends from heaven and we leave revitalized to return to the fray. Our love imitates God's love when we embrace hope, rather than despair, as various situations in our family come to light; for, with God, all things are possible. And our love imitates God's love when we endure all of the difficulties and blessings of the vocation of marriage, knowing that the way of the Cross is the way of life.

If we will yield our hearts and our homes to the Lord, He will show us the path of holiness that runs through our vocation. He will lead us to Himself and show us how we can be together forever as a family with Him. And our magnificent marriage as the Bride of Christ will be reflected in our earthly marriage.

Questions for Discussion

1. How can we help young people who are getting married keep the focus on marriage preparation rather than wedding plans?
2. What is the connection between priority loving and priority living?
3. What are some ways to understand ordinary tasks in a spiritual way?
4. How is marriage connected to the Cross?

Kimberly Hahn is the wife of Scott Hahn and mother of six children. She is one of the authors of the Journey through Scripture *Bible study series for the St. Paul Center and is producing a four volume Bible study series for women called the* Life Nurturing Love *series based on Proverbs 31.*

CHAPTER III

Jesus and the Covenant of Marriage

CURTIS AND STACY MITCH

The longer we are married, the clearer it becomes that we are "one." We have experienced over the years that our personalities and gifts complement one another in so many beautiful ways. When one is weak, the other is strong, and when one is down, the other is there to lift up and encourage. We are sandpaper to one another, each day smoothing out the rough and jagged edges of our souls. Our experience teaches what the Catholic Church teaches, that God has fitted us together to help one another grow in grace toward our heavenly home.

The Lord, as we know, designed married life for this very purpose. But the mission of marriage does not seem this beautiful and clear in the eyes of the world. Time and again the centuries have seen marriage suffer the brutal assaults of human depravity. Adultery, divorce, polygamy, concubinage, homosexual unions—all are corruptions and deviations from the divine plan for married life.

But Christians believe that Jesus Christ redeemed mankind, and, in the process, redeemed the covenant of marriage. The Lord came among us to pull marriage from the wreckage of human sin and to restore its magnificence once again. Our purpose in what follows is to see this miracle in action. The passage for reflection is Matthew 19:1–10.

Marriage in Genesis

The story begins with Jesus on his way to Jerusalem. His ministry in Galilee had come to an end, and the crowds had decided to follow Him on His southward trek to Judea. While Jesus is teaching and healing along the road, the Pharisees approach Him with a theological question: "Is it lawful to divorce one's wife for any cause?" (Mt. 19:3). One might think that the Pharisees are looking for insight into a sensitive legal issue on marriage. But the evangelist indicates otherwise. The question is deliberately framed to test Jesus. The Pharisees, it seems, want to put Jesus into a box and give Him a label. Is He a conservative rabbi or a liberal theologian? Or is He a moderate who stands somewhere in between?

Curiously, Jesus responds not by answering the question directly but by getting at the real issue behind the question. He does this by taking His interrogators back to the beginning of Scripture. Genesis, He reminds them, is the place to look for answers about marriage. There, in the beginning, we see the union of man and women as it was first fashioned by the hands of the Creator. And what does Genesis say? That God "made them male and female" (Mt. 19:4, quoting Gen. 1:27).

Though terse and compact, the passage is heavy with meaning. More than anything, it shows us that God is the Author and Maker of marriage. It is an integral part of His creation. It is part of His design for propagating the human family and bringing couples together in the bonds of human love. Therefore, marriage is not a human institution that is subject to man-made laws and decrees and cultural norms.

The passage also tells us that marriage is heterosexual. The Lord designed it as the intimate union of one man and one woman. Quite literally, Genesis teaches us that man and woman were "made for each other." They are complementary in their sexual, spiritual, and emotional makeup. So when the Lord created the first man and woman, He created a couple rather than two individuals who happened to live at the same place at the same time. In the divine plan, man and woman were meant to share a common life together rather than cross paths occasionally as they went about their separate lives. Genesis 1:27, then, stresses God's role in the creation of marital life. This is the first step toward answering the question of the Pharisees.

Genesis 2:24 is the second step, and this is the passage that Jesus turns to next. The excerpt is an editorial comment made by the Genesis narrator: "For this reason a man shall leave his father and mother and be joined to his wife, and the two shall become one" (Matt. 19:5 quoting Gen. 2:24).[1] Here we learn that the first marriage embodies the divine plan for all marriages. We infer this because, unlike every other groom in the future, the passage doesn't directly apply to Adam! After all, he had no father or mother to pull away from on his wedding day. In any case, the emphasis of the verse is on the "one flesh" union of the marriage partners, and this applies to Adam and Eve and every married couple thereafter.

In the context of Genesis, the oneness of husband and wife can have many levels of significance. Union in "one flesh" is often understood as the sexual intimacy that is proper to married love, and this is, no doubt, part of the meaning. But more is intended. The oneness of a shared life together is also part of the equation, as is the emotional and spiritual oneness that results when spouses give themselves to one another in unselfish generosity.[2] And beyond this, when we situate the passage in its ancient context, we learn that to be one flesh is to be one family. Marriage was considered a covenant in ancient Israel, and covenants created bonds of legal kinship between persons otherwise unrelated.[3]

---

[1] The Greek text of Matthew 19:5, like the Hebrew text of Genesis 2:24, says the two shall become "one flesh" rather than simply "one." It is unclear why the RSVCE abbreviates the translation in this way.

[2] Consider the beautiful words of Pope Pius XI on this point: "By matrimony...the souls of the contracting parties are joined and knit together more directly and more intimately than are their bodies" (*Casti Connubii*, no. 7).

[3] For an explanation of covenant kinship in general as well as its application to the language of "flesh" in Genesis 2:24, see Frank More Cross, *From Epic to Canon: History and Literature in Ancient Israel* (Baltimore: The Johns Hopkins University Press, 1998), 3–21.

Perhaps Jesus intended us to understand all of this from Genesis 2:24. But again, He stresses the divine action that brings about a marriage. When a man and woman consent to be husband and wife, they are truly a couple that "God has joined together" (Mt. 19:6). Sure, the spouses have to give their mutual consent to be married, but Heaven cements the bond between them. So marriage is God's creation, and the union of every married couple is ultimately God's doing.

The implication for the Pharisees' question is stunning. Far from staking out a position on the legitimate grounds for divorce, Jesus says "let no man put asunder" the union of a man and his wife (Mt. 19:6). If God has joined them together, then to break apart a marriage is to break apart God's plan for married life. Divorce, Jesus says, runs directly against the divine plan. It follows that the Lord must have intended marriage to be a lifelong partnership. The marital bond must be a permanent glue that makes the "one flesh" union divinely inseparable. And if "they are no longer two but one" (Mt. 19:6), then husband and wife can't simply divorce and go their separate ways as if they were no longer married in the eyes of God.

Divorce in Deuteronomy

You can almost picture the Pharisees scratching their heads and rubbing their ears when Jesus said, "Let no man put asunder." "Did He just say what I think He said?" they must have whispered to themselves. Not ones to be put down in a public exchange over theology, they are quick to launch a strategic countermeasure: "Why then did Moses command one to give a certificate of divorce, and to put her away?" (Mt. 19:7). This is a reference to the divorce law of Deuteronomy 24:1–4, and on the surface, it appears to be a devastating comeback that pits Jesus against Moses and puts His credibility as a revered rabbi in serious jeopardy. But such is not the case.

Jesus springs back with an ingenious rebuttal that no one saw coming: "For your hardness of heart Moses allowed you to divorce your wives, but from the beginning it was not so" (Mt. 19:8). First, notice that Jesus corrects a subtle misinterpretation of the Pharisees. Moses never "commanded" anyone to put away their wives (Mt. 19:7); he merely "allowed" it to happen in certain cases, Jesus says (Matt. 19:8). Second, Moses only permitted divorce because of Israel's callous and rebellious spirit. It is wrong to think that Moses, when he allowed for divorce, was laying out Yahweh's perfect plan for married life. Far from it. Moses was bending the Law to accommodate a wayward nation. He was lowering the level of moral expectation for a people too weak and too stubborn to live by the high standards of the Lord.

In fact, when we take a closer look at Deuteronomy 24:1–4, we see that it doesn't exactly throw open the doors to divorce and remarriage. The passage assumes that divorce does indeed take place in Israel, and that remarriage often follows on its heels.[4] But divorce and remarriage are actually restricted by Moses rather than encouraged by him. That is, the law of Deuteronomy 24:1–4 is designed to curtail the *abuse* of divorce and remarriage among Israelite men. To paraphrase, Moses says that a divorced couple cannot "remarry" each other once an intervening marriage has taken place. The purpose of this restriction is to make husbands think twice before they make a rash decision to divorce their wives. Why? Because she is likely to get married again, and if she does, he is forbidden to take her back.

More significant for Jesus' exchange with the Pharisees are the cryptic words in Deuteronomy 24:1. Here we have the only mention of the legitimate grounds for divorce in the Mosaic Law. It is defined as "some indecency" (in Hebrew, 'erwat dabar, "nakedness of a thing") that a husband finds displeasing in his wife. What does this mean? Scholars today aren't exactly sure. For that matter, scholars in Jewish antiquity weren't exactly sure either.

Before the time of Jesus, the Book of Sirach took the position that a man was free to divorce his wife for insubordination (Sir. 25:25–26). After the time of Jesus, a ruling by the famed Rabbi Akiba stated that a man could divorce his wife if his affections had diverted to another woman. In Jesus' own day, the question

---

[4] In fact, divorce was taking place in Israel at least 38 years before the Deuteronomic law code was promulgated (see Leviticus 21:7; 22:13).

of divorce was a subject of lively debate within the Pharisaic movement.[5] One school of thought followed the teaching of Rabbi Shammai, and another followed the teaching of Rabbi Hillel. Shammai was the hardline "conservative" who restricted the legitimate grounds for divorce to sexual promiscuity and immodest exposure on the part of a wife. Hillel, by contrast, was the "liberal" who allowed divorce for even the most trivial reasons, such as a wife burning a cooked meal. In the view of most scholars, it is precisely this intramural debate between Shammai and Hillel that the Pharisees set before Jesus. The question of whether a man can divorce his wife "for any cause" (Matt. 19:3) is most likely a tactful way of asking, "Is Hillel right?"[6]

What is striking in light of this background is Jesus' own position on divorce, elucidated by His two quotations from Genesis. Instead of taking sides in the legal debate, backing one rabbi or another, He makes the revolutionary claim that divorce flatly contradicts God's design for marriage. God never wanted it in the first place, so squabbling over the legal grounds for divorce is beside the point. In saying this, Jesus is making a claim that was altogether unheard of in ancient Judaism. He not only raises the standard of marriage above the rabbinic debates, he even revokes the permission to divorce and remarry granted by the Law of Moses.

Jesus' Pronouncement

Now we come to the punch line, to a string of words that rumble like thunder out of the calm. Jesus declares: "And I say to you: whoever divorces his wife, except for unchastity, and marries another, commits adultery" (Mt. 19:9). Here the Lord underscores the awesome sanctity of marriage and the need to guard it against desecration. Unfortunately, it is precisely at this climactic moment that so many interpretations run off the rails. Up to this point,

---

[5] Rabbinic views are summarized in the Mishnaic tractate *Gittin* 9.10. The Mishnah is a compilation of Palestinian Jewish traditions put into writing around AD 200. See also the brief discussion in John P. Meier, *Law and History in Matthew's Gospel*, Analecta Biblica 71 (Rome: Biblical Institute Press, 1976), 143.

[6] This point is made in John A. Hardon, S.J., *The Catholic Catechism* (Doubleday: New York, 1981), 356.

everything seemed to be clear: the Pharisees accept divorce, and even Moses permitted it, but Jesus takes the much stricter view that man must *not* divide what God has joined together. Why, then, does Jesus turn around and make an "exception" to His own ruling? Is He pulling back from the ideal of lifelong marriage to make His difficult teaching more livable?

Many Christians think He was. Protestant groups, and even the Orthodox, appeal to Matthew 19:9 to insist that Jesus allowed for divorce and remarriage in the case of marital infidelity, at least for the innocent spouse.[7] The Catholic Church firmly and rightly rejects this interpretation, and it's important to understand why. Since everything hinges on the so-called "exception clause," we need to look carefully at these few words to understand what Jesus had in mind. It will be helpful to examine several options, for Catholic exegesis has generated three interpretive views to explain the Matthean "exception clause" in a way that is fully consistent with Catholic doctrine on the indissolubility of marriage.

(1) The first is the *Patristic View*, which represents the majority opinion among the early Church Fathers. This view holds that Jesus did, in fact, make an exception that allows for divorce when a spouse is guilty of sexual promiscuity or adultery. However, according to the Fathers, the exception does not allow for remarriage. When a husband and wife divorce, they separate from each other and end their common life together, but the marriage bond endures. Neither is free to remarry until one of the spouses dies. To embark upon a second marriage, before death dissolves the first marriage, is to commit adultery. This view coheres nicely with the grammar of the passage as well as the scope of the word "unchastity," which, in Greek, is an umbrella term for various forms of sexual misconduct.[8]

---

[7] For details, see Timothy Ware, *The Orthodox Church* (Penguin Books: New York, 1997), 295.

[8] Interestingly, one of the best defenders of the Patristic view is a conservative Protestant scholar. For his analysis of the passage, see G.J. Wenham, "Matthew and Divorce: An Old Crux Revisited" *Journal for the Study of the New Testament* 22 (1984), 95–107, and G.J. Wenham, "The Syntax of Matthew 19.9" *Journal for the Study of the New Testament* 28 (1986), 17–23.

(2) The second option is sometimes called the *Consanguinity View*, which is currently popular among various Catholic scholars.[9] According to this interpretation, the exception made for "unchastity" is an exception made for "invalid marriages." The idea is that Jesus is talking about unions between persons too closely related. These are not really marriages at all because they violate the incest laws of Leviticus 18:6–18. A serious impediment is posed by their shared bloodline, and so relatives joined together as couples should indeed separate. Because they were never really married in the first place, they are afterwards free to marry outside their near and immediate families. In support of this view, the Greek term for "unchastity" does refer to incest at times (1 Cor. 5:1), as does its equivalent Hebrew term in the Dead Sea Scrolls (The Damascus Document 5.8–11).

(3) The third option is the *Preteritive View*. It can be traced back to Saint Augustine and has a moderate following today.[10] On this reading of the passage, the exception clause is a "preterition," that is, a parenthetical comment that Jesus uses to set aside the rabbinic debates of Hillel and Shammai over the justifiable grounds for divorce. In effect, it is Jesus' way of refusing to comment on the contemporary disagreements over divorce. The entire legal squabble in Judaism is swept aside as irrelevant to the issue at hand, namely His own teaching on the divine holiness and permanence of Christian marriage.

The Church has not endorsed any one of these views as its "official" interpretation of Matthew 19:9. All are consistent with Catholic teaching on marriage, and so all are permissible interpretations of the passage. The thing to notice is that *none* of the stated views questions the fact that lawful marriage creates an unbreakable bond, that divorce is reserved for extreme situations,

---

[9] E.g., J.A. Fitzmyer, J.P. Meier, F.J. Moloney, etc. The popularity of this view among modern Catholic scholars probably explains why the Consanguinity View is adopted in the New American Bible translation, where the exception clause is rendered "unless the marriage is unlawful" (NAB at Matt. 19:9).

[10] For a defense of the Preteritive View, see Bruce Vawter, C.M., "The Divorce Clauses in Mt 5, 32 and 19, 9" *Catholic Biblical Quarterly* 16 (1954), 155–167, and Bruce Vawter, C. M., "Divorce and the New Testament" *Catholic Biblical Quarterly* 39 (1977), 528–542.

and that remarriage after divorce is never a viable option if the marriage partners are both living.

Confirmation of this comes when we read a little further, for the response of the disciples in the very next verse clinches the case for the Catholic interpretation. In stunned disbelief at the Lord's pronouncement, the disciples come out with a memorable one of their own: "If such is the case of a man with his wife, it is not expedient to marry" (Mt. 19:10). These words would be meaningless if Jesus had just allowed an exception for divorce and remarriage. Every respectable teacher in Judaism allowed for that—Moses, Hillel, Shammai, you name it—and yet no one ever came to the conclusion that it's better to stay single and steer clear of marriage altogether. The disciples' response only makes sense if Jesus has just taken away the parachute that Moses folded into marriage that allowed a man to bail out on his wife with the freedom to find a new one. Thus, if the words of the disciples tell us anything, they tell us that Jesus must have forbidden divorce and remarriage.

The Savior of Marriage

In the end, no one has ever promoted a higher view of marriage than Jesus of Nazareth. Matrimony was certainly esteemed in Judaism, as it has been in various religions and world cultures. But Christ has elevated the union of man and women to a new and sacramental height. He has called us back to the Creator's plan and the bond of a lifelong partnership that belongs to married love. Divorce and remarriage had no place in this original plan, though such things were permitted for a time under the regime of the Old Covenant. Now that the Savior has come, the time for concessions and accommodations is over. Grace is poured out in superabundance to enrich married life and to make married couples living icons of God's unfailing love for the world.

The Church, for her part, continues to give courageous witness to the teaching of Jesus Christ. Though the winds of secularism howl around her and the waves of a selfish world pound against her, she stands firm in supporting the Lord's vision for marriage.

Let's be honest, the gospel of marriage is not an easy standard to live up to; it is a message of long-term commitment and sacrifice. But it's also a message of grace.

Discussion Questions

1. When Jesus discusses marriage, he turns to the creation account in Genesis. What are the lessons he finds in the two passages cited, Genesis 1:27 and 2:24? What is Jesus emphasizing and why?

2. In ancient Judaism, the legality of divorce was taken for granted, as was the fact that divorce included the right to remarry. Where did this idea come from? Does Jesus reaffirm it or revoke it? What are the biblical grounds for his own position? Explain.

3. Many Christians believe that Jesus allowed for divorce and remarriage under certain circumstances. The Catholic Church holds a very different position. What are some ways that a Catholic could help others to understand Jesus' teaching and see the logic of the Church's position? How do the words of the disciples in Matthew 19:10 help us to understand Jesus' meaning in Matthew 19:9?

Curtis Mitch is the co-author, with Dr. Scott Hahn, of the acclaimed Ignatius Study Bible. *He is also a contributing author for the popular* Catholic for a Reason *series (Emmaus Road Publishing).*

Stacy Mitch is author of the best-selling Courageous *series of Bible studies for women published by Emmaus Road Publishing.*

CHAPTER IV

The Sacrament of Marriage as Vocation

REGIS AND LIBBIE FLAHERTY

The grass needs cutting. The youngest needs to be taken to a doctor's appointment. Before dinner, a quick trip to the store is necessary. That leak in the bathroom faucet is getting worse. The car allotment in the budget is already overdrawn for this month. Sound like your family? The individual items might change, but these generally describe the daily trials and adventures of many Catholic families. Life goes by in a rush. Many of us are so busy living our marriages that we can lose sight of the fact that God has a call for us, and the grace to live that call.

Have You Heard the Call?

Vocation is a gracious call from God to a particular way of life—a call which awaits a response. Call and response are central scriptural themes. Sometimes that call, that vocation, is unique to a certain individual, as in the call of Abraham or Moses. At other times, that call is to a people, as when the Decalogue was delivered through Moses at Mount Sinai or when the prophets spoke the words of God to the children of Israel. Nonetheless,

God calls all men and women to freely chose Him and His plan for their lives.

In the New Testament God's call is spoken by the Word Incarnate, Jesus, who calls sinful men and women to follow Him as disciples (Mk. 2:17). He calls them to come to the wedding banquet that he has prepared (Mt. 22:3).

Christ's call and man's response are also a regular theme for Saint Paul.[1] In fact, that call (in Latin, *vocationem*) is pivotal for the Christian. The relationship that results from man's response to Christ's invitation is the foundation of a new life that witnesses to the mercy of God.

Paul writes to the Romans:

> Consider your call (*vocationem*), brethren; not many of you were wise according to worldly standards, not many were powerful, not many were of noble birth; but God chose what is foolish in the world to shame the wise, God chose what is weak in the world to shame the strong, God chose what is low and despised in the world, even things that are not, to bring to nothing things that are. (1 Cor. 1:26–28)

Peter, the rock foundation of the Church, confirms that God has "called us to his own glory and excellence" (2 Pet. 1:3). Again, this is a general call to all men, yet one that requires a personal response. And the call is more than a once in a lifetime decision. It involves an ongoing commitment. "Be . . . zealous to confirm your call and election" (2 Pet. 1:10).

Confirmed in God's Word

The response to the *vocationis* of God has very practical ram-ifications for how life is to be lived. This includes the relationship of man and woman in marriage.[2] From the beginning God called man and woman to a life of unity. It is in the unity of maleness and femaleness that the image of God is found (Gen. 1:27). The first created couple is told: "Be fruitful and multiply, and fill the

---

[1] See Rom. 9:25, 11:29; 2 Thess. 1:11.

[2] See Lk. 16:18; 1 Cor 7:1–7; Eph. 5:21–32; 1 Thess. 4:3–4 and 1 Tim. 4:3–4.

earth and subdue it; and have dominion over the fish of the sea and over the birds of the air and over every living thing that moves upon the earth" (Gen. 1:28). This call was both a blessing and a responsibility.

There are several scriptural examples of married couples who failed to respond to the call of God[3] starting with that first pair, Adam and Eve. Yet, there are also significant examples of married couples who heard God's call and responded. The New Testament extols the faith, obedience, and hospitality of Abraham and Sarah.[4] Tobit and Anna showed heroic virtue as they fed the poor, buried the abandoned dead, clothed the naked, gave alms, prayed, and fasted. Tobias and Sarah showed that God's will was primary in their marriage, as they prayed prior to consummating their union. Tobias declares: "O Lord, I am not taking this sister of mine because of lust, but with sincerity. Grant that I may find mercy and may grow old together with her" (Tob. 8:7).

The married couple, Aquila and Priscilla, are mentioned four times in the New Testament.[5] This couple supported the evangelistic efforts of Saint Paul. They were noted for their hospitality. The local church met in their home (cf. 1 Cor. 16:19). They even "risked their necks for [Paul's] life." In fact, Paul states "to [them] not only I but also all the churches of the Gentiles give thanks" (Rom. 16:3).

But certainly the greatest witness to the value of the vocation of marriage is found in the fact that our Savior was born into a family. The "yes" of both Mary and Joseph to the call (*vocationem*) of God brought the Messiah into their family and into the family of mankind. Surely no couple lived their vocation more fully than Mary and Joseph.

Two That Are One

Since the birth of Christ the Christian family, responding to God's call, has displayed care for the poor and sick, charity to

---

[3] See Jezebel and Ahab, 1 Kings 16–21 and Ananias and Sapphira, Acts 5:1–11.

[4] 1 Pet. 3:5; Heb. 11:8–17.

[5] Acts 18:1; Rom. 16:3, 1 Cor. 16:19, 2 Tim. 4:19.

neighbor, and hospitality to the stranger. Rodney Stark in *The Rise of Christianity* points out that this Christian approach was contrary to the common attitude in the Greco-Roman World. It fact, it was revolutionary. Stark attributes the phenomenal success of the spread of Christianity to the compassion and respect for others that was so evident in Christianity. Even the pagan emperor Julian noted, "that the pagans needed to equal the virtues of Christians" if the old Roman religion was to survive.[6] While Julian tried to legislate morality, the Christians lived it as a free response to God's call to live a holy life.

Rodney Stark further notes that this radical counter-cultural lifestyle was particularly noticeable in marriage. In the typical Roman family, the wife was treated as chattel. Divorce and adultery were normative. Romans practiced contraception, abortion, and infanticide, and had few children. The aged and infirmed were often abandoned and left to die. The Christian family was different. Here monogamy and faithfulness were the standard. Children were welcomed as a blessing from the Lord. "Within the Christian subculture women enjoyed far higher status than did women in the Greco-Roman world at large."[7]

The ancient pagans marveled at this lifestyle. Julian and other emperors of a decaying society wondered how they could convince adherents of the ancient pagan religion to adopt a similar lifestyle. But this way of life was possible only because it was part of the Christian vocation. It was a free response to the call to love God and neighbor. It was possible because it was founded on a cooperation with the grace that God gives to those who seek to follow Him.

A Universal Call

The Second Vatican Council exhorted Catholics to a life and mission that is no less revolutionary than that of those early Christian individuals, families, and communities. The fathers of the Council emphasized the need for a Catholic lifestyle that is

---

[6] Rodney Stark, *The Rise of Christianity* (San Francisco: Harper Collins, 1997), 83.
[7] Stark, *The Rise of Christianity*, 95.

countercultural in a society that shows many of the same evils that plagued ancient Rome. "In the Church, everyone . . . is *called*[8] to holiness, according to the saying of the Apostle: 'For this is the will of God, your sanctification'" (LG, no. 39, emphasis added).

This call, this vocation, to holiness also has an evangelistic component. Not only is personal holiness the goal, it is also a way of life that will impact all of humanity. By personal holiness, God's people "will manifest to all men the love with which God loved the world" (LG, no. 41).

It is within this overarching call to holiness that the basis of marriage as a vocation is found. In marriage, the couple, as one entity, is called to holiness and to an apostolate which springs from a life in service of God and neighbor.

> Married couples and Christian parents should follow their own proper path [to holiness] by faithful love. They should sustain one another in grace throughout the entire length of their lives. They should embue their offspring, lovingly welcomed as God's gift, with Christian doctrine and the evangelical virtues. In this manner, they offer all men the example of unwearying and generous love; in this way they build up the brotherhood of charity; in so doing, they stand as the witnesses and cooperators in the fruitfulness of Holy Mother Church; by such lives, they are a sign and a participation in that very love, with which Christ loved His Bride and for which He delivered Himself up for her. (LG, no. 41)

Another of the Documents of Vatican II, "Decree on the Apostolate of the Laity,"[9] presents the many facets of a married couple's vocation. Husband and wife are to cooperate with God's grace and encourage, support, and give witness of the love of God to each other. As a couple, they "communicate the faith to their children and . . . educate them by word and example."[10]

The Council also reminds the married couple that their vocation is to bear fruit in the world around them. In fact, the Council notes that, particularly in our time, society needs the Christian

---

[8] *Vocantur* in Latin.
[9] *Apostolicam Actuositatem*, November 18, 1965.
[10] *Apostolicam Actuositatem*, 11.

family as a witness to the "indissolubility and sacredness of the marriage bond."[11] In a culture of death, a Catholic family is called to be a beacon of light and a home that proclaims and demonstrates the culture of life.

In the midst of the decaying culture of the later Roman Empire, Catholic families lived in accordance with God's call and saw God's blessing in a flowering of conversion to the Faith. In today's culture a Catholic family as a "domestic sanctuary of the Church" has a mission to be a "vital cell of society." The "Decree on the Apostolate of the Laity" enumerates some of the areas for apostolate by the Catholic family: "the adoption of abandoned infants, hospitality to strangers, assistance in the operation of schools, helpful advice and material assistance for adolescents, help to engaged couples in preparing themselves better for marriage, catechetical work, support of married couples and families involved in material and moral crises, help for the aged . . . by providing them with the necessities of life."[12]

But all of the above are secondary and spring from the centrality of the marriage bond. In living their particular vocation, Catholic couples and families "give effective testimony to Christ before the world by remaining faithful to the Gospel and by providing a model of Christian marriage through their whole life."[13]

The Grace of the Sacrament

The vocation of Christian marriage is a daunting life especially in a culture that is openly hostile to it. Faced with the challenge, it is tempting to say that the task is impossible, as did the Apostles when they received a difficult teaching from Christ (Mt. 19:25). But, as Jesus said to His disciples, He also says to us: "with men this is impossible, but with God all things are possible" (Mt. 19:26).

God is the author of marriage, and man and woman received this gift "from the hand of the Creator" (CCC 1603). Through

---

[11] Ibid.
[12] Ibid.
[13] Ibid.

Christ and His Church, the union of man and wife, already blessed by God, was elevated to the dignity of a sacrament (CCC 1601).

God, a loving Father, gives to man that which is needed for man to respond to His call. When God calls a man and a woman to the covenant of a sacramental marriage, He provides the grace that is needed to live that marriage. All sacraments provide grace and are efficacious when we receive and respond appropriately. There is grace that is particular to the sacrament of Marriage. "This grace proper to the sacrament of Matrimony is intended to perfect the couple's love and to strengthen their indissoluble unity. By this grace they 'help one another to attain holiness in their married life and in welcoming and educating their children'" (CCC 1641). And this grace is available in superabundance because Christ is the source of this grace.

It is God's intent to bless the couple *throughout* their marriage by abiding with those who have invited Him into their lives. The Catechism speaks elegantly of married life with Christ at the center of the relationship:

> Just as of old God encountered his people with a covenant of love and fidelity, so our Savior, the spouse of the Church, now encounters Christian spouses through the sacrament of Matrimony. Christ dwells with them, gives them the strength to take up their crosses and so follow him, to rise again after they have fallen, to forgive one another, to bear one another's burdens, to "be subject to one another out of reverence for Christ," and to love one another with supernatural, tender, and fruitful love. In the joys of their love and family life he gives them here on earth a foretaste of the wedding feast of the Lamb. (CCC 1642)

As the couple cooperates with Christ, the fruit of their vocation blossoms. When they willingly take up the crosses of their life and join them with that of Christ, their love becomes a sign of the love of Christ for His Church (CCC 1615). Pope John Paul II in his Apostolic Letter, *Familiaris Consortio*, states that the grace of the sacrament of Matrimony gives the couple "*power* to live their vocation" (no. 47, emphasis added).

Discernment

Knowing that marriage is a vocation raises the question of how to discern if it is the right vocation for a particular individual.

It is important that every Christian seek God's will for his or her life. God "has very precise plans for each person, a *personal vocation* which each must recognize, accept and develop."[14] The decisions whether to marry and whom to marry are topics for prayer and discernment.

A detailed discussion on how to discern a vocation is beyond the scope of this chapter, but a brief overview is possible. First, the person seeking God's will for his or her life should approach the question with confidence. God desires that His people would know His will for them. Therefore, fear is inappropriate. The words that God spoke to His people in exile through the prophet Jeremiah should fill us with hope:

> For I know the plans I have for you, says the LORD, plans for welfare and not for evil, to give you a future and a hope. Then you will call upon me and come and pray to me, and I will hear you. You will seek me and find me; when you seek me with all your heart, I will be found by you, says the LORD." (Jer. 29:11–14)

A desire for personal holiness is another prerequisite for hearing God's call. This involves a commitment to living a full Christian life with a willingness to do *whatever* God wants. Communication is necessary to both hear a call and respond. So regular committed prayer is essential. The sacraments, especially Eucharist and Reconciliation, open the receptive individual to God's work and direction. Guidance of parents, a spiritual director, and those "older" in the faith can help in discernment.

Chaste and holy relations with the opposite sex are important. "Physical expressions of affection [during courtship] must be brief, prudent and chaste. Seeking sexual satisfaction is not only wrong in itself but self-defeating, for it derails the process of

---

[14] The Pontifical Council for the Family, *Truth and Meaning of Human Sexuality* (December 8, 1995), no. 100. (Emphasis in the original).

discernment."[15] Courtship is to be a time for the couple to discern if God is drawing them to marriage with one another. Honesty and self-disclosure are vital attitudes in the process.

After marriage, the couple must continue to discern God's will. Any and all decisions should be made in the context of vocation and God's gracious call. Does this new job prospect support my vocation as a married person or does it detract from it? Is this change in housing the best option for us as a Catholic family? Will this decision help us to be better spouses and parents or will it be detrimental? The life of the Catholic is to be ordered in faith, hope, and charity to the fulfillment of God's call. We "are obliged to organize our lives in their entirety in a way that supports and contributes to the carrying-out of our vocational commitments."[16]

Married life will inevitably have its times of difficulty and trial. It is important, especially in trying times, for the couple to recall that God has called them to this life. Commitment, reliance upon the grace of the Sacrament, and fidelity are essential to living a vocation. At times, a reexamination of priorities and repentance may be necessary. Reliance upon God and love for each other can weather many storms. "Hope makes it possible to accept the painful things that can't be changed as elements in God's plan."[17]

In the midst of particular circumstances there can be confusion, but the couple need only look to our Savior to gain perspective. As the author of Hebrews tells us, "let us . . . persevere in running the race that lies before us while keeping our eyes fixed on Jesus, the leader and perfecter of faith. For the sake of the joy that lay before him he endured the cross, despising its shame, and has taken his seat at the right of the throne of God" (Heb. 12:12 NAB). Heaven is our goal, and the eternal life promised by Him who died and rose gives us a hope that endures.

---

[15] Germain Grisez and Russell Shaw, *Personal Vocation, God Calls Everyone by Name* (Huntingdon, IN: Our Sunday Visitor, 2003), 104.
[16] Grisez and Shaw, *Personal Vocation*, 110.
[17] Ibid., 113.

It Is in the Living

In ending this discussion we want to address those who did not seek God's will when they were considering marriage or a marriage partner and may even believe that they chose outside of God's will. Have these couples and individuals missed God's plan for their lives? Are they relegated to some second place because of past failings or lack of knowledge?

To address this question, moral theologian Germain Grisez points out that even if we are unfaithful, God is faithful. Even if we leave Him, He is waiting for our return. We may be wayward children, but He is always a faithful Father. Our failings and our sins cannot outdo God's promise and plan.

So God calls that wife or that husband to respond to Him where they are. "Although a sinner may miss his vocation, a repentant sinner once more has a complete personal vocation."[18] There may be particular struggles because of wrong choices and sin. Our actions do have consequences, but no one should underestimate God's mercy and love.

On the cross beside Jesus on Calvary hung a thief, someone who had made bad choices in his life. Yet, in repentance, he turned to Jesus who forgave him and promised glory. The thief still died upon the cross—a consequence of his sin. However, that same day he joined his Savior in paradise (Lk. 23:42–43). No matter where we are in a marriage, we can always turn to Jesus. The grace of the Sacrament remains available, provided we remain free of mortal sin.

Conclusion

The Roman world was changed from paganism to Christendom partly because Catholic men and women lived their marriages in holiness and as a response to the call of Christ. The best weapons against the forces of evil and the culture of death in our day are Catholic couples and families who embrace Catholic marriage

---

[18] Germain Grisez, *Living a Christian Life* (Quincy, IL: Franciscan Press, 1993), 118.

and show the world the reflected light of Jesus, against which darkness flees.

Family life in our society is often hectic. But for the Catholic couple there is a call and a grace that makes a world of difference.

Discussion Questions

1. What is your understanding of vocation? What is the difference between the call given to all Christians and a "personal vocation"?
2. What does the grace of the sacrament of Matrimony offer to a married couple? (see CCC 1641–1642 and 2225). How can a couple dispose themselves to receive that grace?
3. How can a person discern the vocation to which God calls him or her?
4. Do you agree that Catholic marriage and family can be a great light in our culture? How so?

Regis and Libbie Flaherty teach pre-marriage classes and a marriage enrichment course, which they developed, in the Diocese of Pittsburgh. They have been the featured speakers for a World Marriage Day celebration in Pittsburgh and have written a marriage enrichment brochure, which is given to couples when they prepare for the Baptism of a child.

Regis is Editor-in-Chief of Emmaus Road Publishing and a frequent contributor to Catholic periodicals. He has written several books including Last Things First *(Our Sunday Visitor) and* Catholic Customs: A Fresh Look at Traditional Practices *(Servant).*

CHAPTER V

Lessons
Learned at Nazareth
Living the Example of
the Holy Family

MIKE AND GWEN SULLIVAN

A s parents of seven children, we often get the feeling that we are living on a different planet. People gawk at us when we are out in public. We routinely hear negative comments from strangers. Some of the comments include: "Are those *all* yours?"; "Don't you have a television?"; or, our favorite, "You must be Mormons." We've learned to laugh off such questions, but the fact that we hear them so often makes us realize just how far our society has gone in its outright opposition to the family.

This opposition to the family is especially disturbing, as the family has always formed the basic core around which communities are built. The family, according to Vatican II, is "the first and vital cell of society."[1] The Council also said that the well-being of individuals and even society "is closely bound up with the healthy state of conjugal and family life" (GS, no. 47).

So what is a family to do in today's age when trying to live the Christian life is an affront to the secular society in which we live? This is a difficult question, but it is one that has been

---

[1] Second Vatican Council, Decree on the Apostolate of the Laity *Apostolicam Actuositatem* (November 18, 1965), no. 11.

asked many times in many ages before ours. Think of the early Christians, living under Roman persecution, who clandestinely met for the sacraments in caves under the city. If they were discovered they'd surely be tortured, mutilated, or murdered. Consider also the plight of Catholics in many places during the Protestant Reformation when Mass was outlawed and Catholics were regularly imprisoned and murdered.

Throughout history, Catholics have struggled against the world. In these times, "the saints have always been the source and origin of renewal in the most difficult moments in the Church's history" (CCC 828). The one guiding principle for families has always been to accept the challenge and respond to the world aggressively by striving for holiness.

What better example do we have as Christian families than to model our lives after the family *par excellence*, the Holy Family?

By reflecting on the roles of Mary as mother, Joseph as father, and Jesus as child, we can gain a spiritual perspective that continuously shapes our understanding of our roles in our own families. In our own family we've tried to reflect on these various roles of the Holy Family and we were blessed to find some helpful comments by Pope Paul VI.

Nazareth

While on pilgrimage to Nazareth, Pope Paul VI reflected, "Nazareth is a kind of school. . . . How I would like to return to my childhood and attend the simple yet profound school that is Nazareth!" He went on to explain that there are three key lessons to learn by reflecting on Christ's childhood in Nazareth.

- First, he said we learn from its silence: "We need this wonderful state of mind," he said, to combat the pressures and noise of the world.
- Second, he said that Nazareth serves as "a model of what the family should be . . . a community of love and sharing, beautiful for the problems it poses and the rewards it brings, in sum, the perfect setting for rearing children—and for this there is no substitute."

- Finally, he said, "[I]n Nazareth, the home of a craftsman's son, we learn about work and the discipline it entails." (Office of Readings, December 26)

As Christian parents, we are called to model our own family life after that of the Holy Family in Nazareth. By shaping our homes in the example of silence, community love, and discipline, we ensure that we are doing our part in establishing a nurturing environment in which saints are made. Let us examine each of these areas and consider how we might apply them to family life.

Silence

It is no surprise that Pope Paul VI mentions silence as his first reflection on the life of the Holy Family at Nazareth, for it is in silence that we are trained in prayer. It is also in interior silence that we contemplate and have communion with God. A "silent" interior life is one free of distraction: it is a life of constancy. The "noise" of the world disrupts and distracts us.

In our home, there is very little "silence." Just imagine seven children under the age of eleven, praying, playing, learning, working, and occasionally, fighting. But we try our best to limit outside distractions and influences. We don't watch television, but we do occasionally watch wholesome movies. The children are allowed to listen to music only if it is edifying. Playtime with friends is limited. We do our best to form a family culture that is particular to our own family, one that is focused on the character formation and education of our children.

Archbishop Chaput once said, "We need to unplug a little from the network of noise that surrounds us. We need to create the room for a silence that we can fill with conversation—conversation with each other and with God."[2]

The time we have to form and help build virtue in our children is short; we must make the best of it. They too will leave the home

---

[2] See online at http://www.archden.org/archbishop/docs/family_society_090501.htm.

and go about the will of the Father. They need our protection and nurturing in order to grow into the saints they are called to be. By limiting negative influences from outside the home, we provide the kind of environment that fosters good character formation and peace in our home.

As Pope Paul VI said,

> The silence of Nazareth should teach us how to meditate in peace and quiet, to reflect on the deeply spiritual, and to be open to the voice of God's inner wisdom and the counsel of his true teachers. Nazareth can teach us the value of study and preparation, of meditation, of a well-ordered personal spiritual life, and of silent prayer that is known only to God.

We don't know much from Scripture about Jesus' childhood. But when we consider what we do know, it is clear that the Holy Family's home in Nazareth was a sanctuary, set apart from the distractions and influence of the world. For Christ, it was a time marked by hidden formation and preparation for His mission. Remember that, for Jesus, preparation in the quiet of Nazareth was so important that it represents thirty of His thirty-three years spent on this earth!

Our homes should be similar sanctuaries, hidden from the world. The more negative influences we allow into our homes, the less control we have over what is forming the character of our children. A home marked by silence is a home where the priorities are straight. There is a focus on the spiritual good of the children and an avoidance of the distractions of the world.

By fostering silence in the home, we teach our children to avoid distraction. They will be able to concentrate better, and thus will be more attuned to develop their faith. Blessed Teresa of Calcutta explained how she and her sisters were aware of God's will for them. She said, "Before you speak, it is necessary for you to listen, for God speaks in the silence of the heart." By fostering silence in the home our children will learn to pray and develop a loving relationship with God, with each other, and with us. But this ideal is difficult to realize.

There are many circumstances that even the most experienced parents find overwhelming. In our family life, sometimes we just don't know what we are supposed to do in certain situations. We often struggle with decisions about our children's education or how to handle certain disciplinary problems. In these instances, reflecting on Mary's struggles can be very helpful. In Luke's Gospel, we see several instances of Mary's "pondering heart." She wasn't sure what to make of the events unfolding in her life but she trusted in God's providence and pondered these things in the silence of her heart (see Lk. 1:28, 2:19, and 2:51). As parents, there are many things we don't understand as we strive to raise our children in accord with God's will. But if we ponder these questions and lift them up to God in prayer, we will soon understand what He is calling us to do.

Community of Love and Sharing

Pope Paul VI called Nazareth the "model of what the family should be." He went on to say that building a "community of love and sharing" is crucial to teaching children the virtues. It is also necessary to form within them the raw material for selfless, loving relationships with God and with their future spouse and children.

Building a community of love and sharing begins with each family member's willingness to offer him or herself for the sake of another. We parents are called to be the first examples of this self-giving. In our home, we do our best to provide a good example of self-giving for the children. We have a chore list with jobs for each child. Sometimes, when the work is really difficult, we will all pitch in and help the child whose chore is especially daunting. The children learn from this example and the older children will often kick in and help their younger siblings to tie their shoes or tidy the bathroom.

But the self-giving we are called to is much more than just our work. The spirit in which our work is done is what is important. Our lives are to be ordered to the joyful service of others. Think of the self-giving of the Holy Family. Mary understood this.

Consider how she dropped everything and traveled to visit her cousin Elizabeth. Even though she was pregnant herself, Mary willingly and happily went and served the needs of her elder cousin (see Lk. 1:39–56).

Consider Mary's role in suffering through her Divine Son's torture and death on the Cross. She knew that she and her Son would have great sufferings to endure, but she humbly and loving embraced her call and remained at His side until His death.

Likewise, Saint Joseph offered an example of total self-surrender when he humbly accepted God's will in leading his family out of danger into Egypt (see Mt. 2:13–15). They would flee as refugees, in poverty. But it was God's will. It was what they had to do to protect the Divine Child.

We as parents must be prepared to drop everything and flee in order to protect our family. This applies not only to bodily protection, but most importantly to the protection of our souls. When we perceive a threat to the moral life of our family, we must flee from that threat or root it out of our homes. If we wish to build a community of love and sharing, we must first look after those in our charge and provide a protective environment in which they might develop.

Discipline

Mary and Joseph educated Jesus, and Joseph taught Him to work as a carpenter. We live in a very different time, and it is uncommon that both parents are able to teach their children by working with them throughout each day. These lessons about hard work and discipline are just as important and can be learned when parents simply make the effort to allow their children to help them in their daily tasks at home. By helping their parents, children learn the virtues of diligence, self-discipline, and responsibility. They also learn the value of work.

In addition to these other virtues, children learn obedience. Obedience to the parents' will is a training exercise for obedience to the will of the Father. As Saint Luke tells us, after the finding of the Child Jesus in the temple, even Jesus himself "was obedient to them" and "increased in wisdom and in stature, and in favor with God and man" (Lk. 2:51–52). Obedience fosters the virtue of humility, which is the foundation of all virtues, and which, with love, forms the core of holiness. We all know that our children are not perfect; their souls, like our own, have been stained by original sin. This is why discipline is critical in fostering holiness in our family.

The word discipline comes from the Latin word *disciplina*, which means instruction or knowledge, which comes from the word for "disciple." God gives parents the duty to discipline their children. As parents, we are accountable to God for their souls and their formation. We are called to instruct them in virtue. Pope Pius XI called parents the "vicars of Christ" in the home. So we are called to bring Christ to our children and form them in the faith. It is important to keep discipline positive, and remember that it is through discipline that we form our children's character. Children cannot learn virtue without the guidance and example of self-giving parents.

Prayer

In Pope Paul VI's reflections on Nazareth, he discussed silence, the family as a community of love and sharing, and discipline. What ties these distinctive features of the Holy Family together is *prayer*. Prayer is rooted in interior silence; it is the core of a community of love and sharing, and it gives rise to discipline. If we have a relationship with God, we pray. It is that simple. In modeling our families after the Holy Family, prayer must be the center of our lives and our greatest priority. If we wish to be holy families, we must pray. Holiness is our greatest weapon against the influences of the world and it is our most persuasive argument for sharing our Christian faith.

The Holy Family's life in Nazareth was one steeped in Scripture. For instance, Mary's Magnificat (see Lk. 1:46–55) shows a thorough knowledge of Scripture. It draws from many books of the Bible and is spontaneously strung together in such a beautiful way that it is clear that she had a profound knowledge of the meaning of that which she spoke. The words were hers, but she was quoting diverse passages with ease, making them her own. Likewise, Christ Himself quoted Scripture with ease and almost constantly throughout the New Testament.

Daily readings of Scripture in our homes or, better yet, participating in the Church's Liturgy of the Hours, should hold a place of prominence in Catholic homes. In fact, the Holy See has taught that praying the Liturgy of the Hours helps families to fully live the life of the Church: "It is fitting . . . that the family, as a domestic sanctuary of the Church, should not only offer prayers to God in common, but also, according to circumstances, should recite parts of the Liturgy of the Hours, in order to be more intimately linked with the Church."[3] While we do not read the Liturgy of the Hours as a family every day, on feast days or solemnities we often read the evening prayer and readings or sing the hymns of the given day. This connects us to the liturgical year and teaches the children that we are part of the Universal Church in its daily prayers and liturgical seasons.

For our family, we have found that Scripture grounds our children in the faith. The stories from Scripture are embedded deeply in the children's minds. In our situation, with seven children under the age of eleven, it is difficult to retain the children's attention when reading Scripture. But we do our best to make up for this by singing songs and praying the Rosary while emphasizing scriptural stories and phrases. It is easy to be discouraged, and we wonder if we are adequately forming our children in the faith. But we've found that prayerfully reflecting on the mysteries of the Rosary teaches our kids to pray and opens their minds to the stories in Scripture.

According to Pope Paul VI, "there is no doubt that . . . the Rosary should be considered as one of the best and most efficacious prayers in common that the Christian family is invited to recite."[4] The Rosary can't be overestimated in its usefulness as a tool for catechesis.

---

[3] Institutio Generalis de Liturgia Horarum, no. 118.

[4] Pope Paul VI, Apostolic Exhortation for the Right Ordering and Development of Devotion to the Blessed Virgin *Mary Marialis Cultus* (February 2, 1974), no. 54.

We often invite door-to-door missionaries or Jehovah's Witnesses to come into our home for a meal or simply for discussion. Once we had a couple of young Mormon missionaries over for dinner. We prayed together and talked, and after our meal, they sat with the children and talked about Jesus.

One of the missionaries asked our then-four-year-old daughter Molly if she loved Jesus. "Oh, yes," she replied, and went on to talk about the life of Jesus. She told how "Jesus' mommy talked to an angel," and then became "the Mommy of God." She excitedly told how Mary visited Elizabeth, "because she had a baby in her tummy, too, and Mary helped her. Her baby was John Baptist." Molly told how Jesus was born in a manger in Bethlehem, how Simeon told Mary she was going to be sad about Jesus' death, and that "her heart would be pierced by a sword." She continued and told how Mary and Joseph found Jesus in the Temple "teaching the teachers."

The Mormon missionaries were amazed. We were amazed. Our four-year-old daughter had just explained the major points of Jesus' early life with profound clarity and understanding. We realized for the first time how the Rosary is much more than simply a prayer. It is a way to drink in the beauty of Scripture that even a four-year-old can understand.

Children learn best from stories and personal experiences. If we as parents expose our children to stories about the lives of the saints and give them opportunities to experience the beauty of their faith, these formational moments will be deeply written upon their memories. They will learn from the stories of the Child Jesus about how to act, how to obey, how to love, and how to pray. By creating our own little Nazareth, today's families can imbibe the lessons of the Holy Family and become solidly rooted in the virtues that build up the family and the world.

Our world today is so divorced from the simplicity of the Holy Family that it is difficult to stay the course in living the Christian life. But it is possible. We are called to be in the world, not of the world. If we hold up the Holy Family as the example for our families, we will learn how to live holy lives and we will begin to change even the culture in which we live. Our little Nazareth will be the refreshing and silent sanctuary we all seek to enter each day as we become disciplined and prayerfully work toward our common goal in a community of love and sharing.

Discussion Questions

1. In what ways could we modify our family routine to better reflect the life of the Holy Family?
2. Reflecting on the scripture passages about Mary's "pondering heart," how might we better prayerfully contemplate the trials and struggles in our own family life?
3. When Joseph received the message from the angel that he was to take the Christ child and His mother to Egypt (see Mt. 2:13–15), he followed the command in order to protect Jesus from Herod. In what ways might parents protect their children from the things of the world that threaten the family?
4. How might we give support or encouragement to families we know or see in public?
5. What lessons are to be learned from reflecting on the life of the Holy Family as an example of silence, as a community of love and sharing, and discipline?

Mike and Gwen Sullivan write from Toronto, Ohio, where they live with their seven children.

Mike is Vice-President of Catholics United for the Faith and Editor-in-Chief of Lay Witness *magazine.*

CHAPTER VI

The Priesthood
of the Laity in the
Domestic Church

H. LYMAN STEBBINS

This Friday in September we keep as a kind of echo of Good Friday, as the day when the soul of Our Lady was pierced by the sword of sorrow, as the Heart of Her Son was pierced by the lance.[1] I beg them to accept this little offering as parents lovingly accept even the most absurd drawings and scribblings from their small children.

Today, the theme of our National Congress is focused on "The Sacred Heart of Jesus, Source of Peace and Reconciliation in the Home," while the topic assigned for this opening talk is "The Priesthood of the Laity in the Domestic Church." Those are very large topics indeed. Perhaps the most useful thing I can hope to do today is simply to explore the terms of my title. First: What is priesthood? What, then, is the priesthood of the laity? What do the words mean to us personally and practically? What dignity do they suggest, what obligations do they imply? Second:

---

[1] This talk was delivered by H. Lyman Stebbins, founder and former president of Catholics United for the Faith, at the National Sacred Heart Congress, Hazelton, PA on September 15, 1978. The topic is as timely today as it was in 1978. Mr. Stebbins died in February of 1989.

What are we saying when we refer to the family and the home as a Church in miniature, a domestic Church? And finally: What practical consequences should flow from the connection between the idea of the priesthood of the laity and the idea of the home as a little Church?

I

First, then, what is priesthood in general? It can be described as the state of being committed—by assignment and by choice—to the service of God in worship, sacrifice, and prayer and mediation between God and men by sacrifice, service, and teaching. Saint Thomas Aquinas says that the work of the priest can be summed up in one sentence: "He is to stand between God and the people. The chief act by which the priest accomplishes his office as mediator has always been the act of sacrifice . . . the wider sense of sacrifice includes all that is offered to God that the spirit of men may be lifted up to God."[2] The whole story of our redemption is the story of the sacrifice and service of Jesus Christ, the God-man and Supreme High Priest: the daily, hourly sacrifice and "doing good" found in the life which Christ lived among us, leading up to the unique, supreme, perfect sacrifice of the death He died among us.

Now, it is a certain truth of our faith that the sacrifice by the God-man was sufficient and unique and was the work of Jesus alone, but it is also a certain truth that, by Holy Orders, men are called and set apart to perpetuate that oblation, as "other Christs," in the Holy Sacrifice of the Mass. And it is a further certain truth that, by Baptism, in an analogous, but essentially different mode, we are all called to share in that act of offering with Christ the Priest and in that act of being offered with Christ the Victim.

It is not always sufficiently realized that all of us have this priestly character, but a chorus of the early Fathers attests to the great fact: "What is the people itself but priestly?" asks

[2] Walter Farrell, O.P., *A Companion to the Summa: The Way of Life* (corresponding to *Theologica* III A and Supplement) (New York: Sheed and Ward, 1942), 120.

Saint Ambrose; "Everyone is anointed to the priesthood" (*On the Sacraments*, 4, 1, 3). Saint Augustine teaches: "As we call all believers Christians on account of the mystical chrism, so we call all priests because they are members of the one Priest" (*The City of God*, 20, 10). Saint Isidore echoes the same teaching: "The whole Church is consecrated by the unction of chrism, because each is a member of the eternal King and Priest" (*On the Offices of the Church*, 2, 26). And so it has continued on through Pope Pius XII's *Mediator Dei* and the Second Vatican Council. And all is based, of course, on Holy Scripture, on Saint Peter who wrote: "You are a chosen generation, a kingly priesthood, a holy nation." (1 Pet. 2:9[3]); and on Saint John who wrote: "Jesus Christ . . . hath loved us and washed us from our sins in his own blood and hath made us a kingdom and priests to God and his Father" (Rev. 1:5, DR). Evidently we do all bear the burden and the glory of what is sometimes called the priesthood of the baptized, but let me stress again that that does not mean that we all share in the special, ordained, sacramental priesthood conferred by Holy Orders. That is a different burden and a greater glory, indicated by Saint Francis who is quoted by Thomas of Celano as saying, "If I were to meet in the same moment one of the blessed come down from heaven, and a poor priest, I should go first to the priest in order to honor him, and I should hasten to kiss his hands because they handle the Word of Life" (*Legenda* 2, pt. 2).

In the Holy Sacrifice of the Mass we have a paradox identical to that of Calvary. There, at the altar, the ordained priest alone, the representative of Christ Himself, offers the sacrifice, and yet we all share in the offering. This great truth is carefully protected by the Latin text of the Mass in our Roman rite. For instance, in the *Orate, fratres,* we have: "Pray, brethren, that my sacrifice— and yours—may be made acceptable to God the almighty Father." Who can fail to be reminded of the words of Our Savior: "I ascend to my Father and to your Father, to my God and your God" (Jn. 20:17, DR). It is a pity that this important nuance is

---

[3] This scripture is taken from the Douay-Rheims Bible. Hereafter identified as "DR."

slurred over in our English version to read simply "our sacrifice," as if there were no distinction.

It is so necessary to understand the importance of the office as such. If I discover a small blaze near some wooden buildings and extinguish it, as it is my civic duty to do, that does not make me a member of the fire department. If I overcome a bandit in the sub-way—a very small and kindly bandit, please God!—that does not make me a policeman. Similarly, we all have the general priestly *function* of offering sacrifice, glorifying God, and serving neighbor in our state of life, though we are not endowed with the *office* of doing so on behalf of the entire community. It is interesting that, to the man who *is* ordained to fill that office on behalf of the whole community, we give the same name that we give to the head of a family. We call him "Father." Naturally, it would be absurd to say that he is just like any other father except that he has more children. No, the fatherhood of the ordained priest is also named after the divine paternity, but it is different in kind, not just in degree, from the fatherhood of a family. The ordained priesthood itself is different in kind from the priesthood of the baptized.

But the point here is that there *is* this priesthood of the bap-tized; it is a teaching of the Church, and it entails certain personal and practical obligations. These obligations arise first and especially in the home. So, before considering what they may be, let us look at the second focus of our subject: the family, the home, viewed as a Church in miniature.

II

That phrase may have a strange ring in some modern ears; but it is ancient, and if it sounds strange to us, the source of the difficulty may be largely in ourselves. *The Dogmatic Constitution on the Church* says (no. 11):

> From the marriage of Christians there comes the family in which new citizens of human society are born and, by the grace of the Holy Spirit in Baptism, these are made children of God so that the People of God may be perpetuated throughout the centuries. In what might be regarded as *the domestic Church,*

the parents by word and example are the heralds of the faith with regard to their children.

It is a striking and important thought. The ultimate meaning of the home is as a school of sanctity, a nursery of vocations. The ultimate mission of the parents is to cooperate with the Holy Spirit in developing their own children into children of God whose first duty and joy it may be to spread the kingdom of God on earth and to enter it in heaven. But what is the ultimate meaning and mission of the Church itself? The Council tells us (*The Decree on the Apostolate of Lay People*, no. 2) that it is "to spread the kingdom of Christ all over the earth for the glory of God the Father, to make all men partakers of redemption and salvation." Words applied officially to the family can often be applied, with perfect appropriateness, to the Church—and *vice versa*. And this is not a unique case.

For instance, some of the ancients among us will remember the beautiful *Asperges me,* chanted immediately before the principal Sunday Mass, while the celebrant sprinkled the altar, the clergy, and the people to prepare them, by this purification, to take part worthily in the Holy Sacrifice. It may not be well known to all that Holy Church there put on the lips of the celebrant the very same prayer which she has appointed for one of the blessings of a home! We may be grateful indeed that this prayer of blessing very significantly has its place before the Mass for the Enthronement of the Sacred Heart in the home, and thereby brings together the two strands of my topic.

Our own immediate families constitute the first mission field for the exercise of the priesthood of the baptized. It is there that the parents have the mission to teach, sanctify, and rule. Even if I tried, I could not invent words to express the sublimity of that mission more strikingly than recent popes have done. Pope Pius XI, in his encyclical *Casti Connubii* on Christian Marriage, said:

> Christian parents must also understand that they are destined . . . to propagate and . . . educate . . . children who are to become members of the Church of Christ, to raise up fellow-citizens of

the saints, and members of God's household, that the worshippers of God and Our Savior may daily increase. . . . Both husband and wife . . . receiving these children with joy and gratitude from the hand of God, will regard them as a talent [Please note that word!] committed to their charge by God, not only to be employed for their own advantage or for that of an earthly commonwealth, but to be restored to God with interest on the day of reckoning.

In his encyclical *Divini Ilius Magistri* on Christian Education, the same Pontiff wrote:

In the first place the Church's mission of education is in wonderful agreement with that of the family, for both proceed from God, and in a remarkably similar manner. . . . The Angelic Doctor . . . says: "The father according to the flesh has in a particular way a share in that principle which in a manner universal is found in God. The Father is the principle of generation, of education and discipline and of everything that bears upon the perfection of human life" (*Summa Theologica* 2–2, Q. C II, a I). The family therefore holds directly from the Creator the mission and hence the right to educate the offspring, a right inalienable *because* inseparably joined to a strict obligation, a right anterior to any right whatever of civil society and of the State, and therefore inviolable on the part of any power on earth. (nos. 13 and 15, emphasis added)

Although the Pope roots the unquestionable authority of the father in the divine authority, he points out that the principle extends to both parents, saying later in the same encyclical: "Parents, therefore, and all who take their place in the work of education, should be careful to make right use of the authority given them by God, whose *vicars* in a true sense they are" (*Divini Ilius Magistri*, no. 74, emphasis added).

Pope John XXIII in his encyclical *Ad Petri Cathedram* (On Truth, Unity and Peace in a Spirit of Charity), on June 29, 1959, repeated the same teaching:

Let the father of the family take the place of God among his children, and not only by his authority but by the upright example of his life also stand clearly in the first place. Let the mother, however, rule firmly over her offspring by gentleness and virtue

in the domestic setting. Let her behave with indulgence and
love towards her husband and, along with him, let her carefully
instruct and train her family. (nos. 53–54)

We really must notice with astonishment, and take to heart,
that here two divinely appointed Vicars of Christ on earth
are telling fathers of families that *they* are God's vicars in the
domestic Church! They, with their wives, have the priestly office
there, but the office of the father is of higher authority. He is to
be aware, first of all, that, like the universal Vicar of Christ, the
assignment implies being the servant of all. He is to be the one
on whom the child can build his idea of Our Father in heaven:
neither a stern master, nor an easy mark. Thus the father's task
needs not only strength, but tenderness, justice, humility, and
purity. Saint Joseph was the least of the Holy Family, but he was
the head of it!

It is a glory and a burden for us that the dignity of the laity
in the Church has received such recognition, but we have to take
care. It often happens that people who have been eager in seeking
to establish their rights turn out to be lazy in their exercise of them.
Our newly affirmed rights require of us both zeal and humility.
Unhappily, the zeal, not infrequently, expresses itself as what
Saint Benedict called the "evil zeal of bitterness which separates
from God and leads to hell,"[4] while the so-called humility is often
merely a false title for lovelessness and indolence.

Without a doubt, many parents today have suffered grievously
at the hands of an immature and elitist we-group who, brandishing
in each hand an academic certificate in something-or-other, feel
haughtily superior to the mother who is rocking the baby with
one hand and doing the dishes with the other. But just the
same, it is regrettable that so many such parents then, under
the impression that they are exhibiting good zeal, carry about a
huge anger against the sisters or brothers or priests who are not
properly forming the children in the faith as it has come down
to us from the Apostles, and was proclaimed by Pope Paul VI in

---

[4] *The Rule of Saint Benedict*, chap. 72.

his *Credo of the People of God.* We get a better perspective if we remember that twenty-five years ago the usual problem was not this unholy anger but an unholy indifference among the parents. How many of today's parents and grandparents are aware that Pope Pius XII felt obliged to warn publicly that the children were not being properly instructed *at home!*

Pope Pius XII asked:

> Why is it that such great efforts on the part of teachers, so many hours and years of constant dedication sometimes show almost no results, if not that the *family,* with its educational lapses, its pedagogical errors and its bad example day by day destroys whatever the teacher tries so laboriously to build? . . . Families should not be allowed to believe that they have satisfied their duties towards their children when they have sent them off to school, giving no thought to working hand in hand with the teachers, on whom they *wrongly* think they can completely unload a part of their responsibilities. (Address to Italian Catholic Union of Middle-School Teachers, January 4, 1954)

We do not need a calculator to reckon that teachers who are, without doubt, often shortchanging the children today are themselves, in many cases, the children of parents who thus shortchanged *them!* The sins of the fathers are visited upon the children even unto the third and fourth generation! Indeed! What earthly good does it do then (certainly it does no heavenly good!) for us parents to be accusing them angrily when God Himself is patiently accusing us, asking us as He asked Saint Peter, "What is that to you? Do your own task by following Me!" (cf. Jn. 21:22).

III

That brings me now to the third and final part of this talk. What *is* our task? What are the practical implications for us laymen of these ideas of the priesthood of the laity and of the home as a little Church? One thing seems sure: we have to fear if we don't reform. Who can doubt that this post-conciliar period is, for us, a time of God's visitation? We recall how the Sacred Heart of Jesus was moved to tears over Jerusalem because she had not

understood the things that were for her peace, had not known
the time of her visitation, and because, in consequence, "now
they are hidden from thine eyes" (Lk. 19:42, DR). Awful words!
We of the laity must strive to see these things while we have the
light of day. Who knows how long the light will last! Long ago,
Saint Augustine warned us—warned us lay people in 1978—that
we must either reform or greatly fear:

> You have heard in the Gospel the punishment of the servant
> who buried his talent, whereas God is covetous with regard to
> salvation. We bishops stand in God's place; we look for splen-
> did profit in your lives. . . . And this office of putting out to use
> [that is, investing at interest] belongs also in its measure to you
> of the laity. You cannot, indeed, execute it from this elevated seat
> [of the episcopacy] but you can wherever you chance to be . . .
> discharge your office in your own house! A bishop is so called
> *because* he takes care of and attends to others. To every man,
> then, if he is head of his own house, the office of the Episcopacy
> ought to belong: to take care how the members of his household
> believe, that none of them fall into heresy . . . because they have
> been bought at so great a price . . . If you do this, you will be
> putting out to use; you will not be slothful servants, you will
> not have to fear so horrible a condemnation! (Saint Augustine,
> *Sermon 44* on Mt. 25:24–30)

We seem to be offered the choice between two terrors! It is
fearful to think of being condemned as a rash servant, so a man
may argue internally: "I just do not want to take any risks with what
is not ultimately my own. I think I should be cautious above all,
aiming only to get by without any kind of blame, quite unnoticed
as is befitting a poor humble soul like me. But now he's telling me
that I must take on an office like an important man—indeed, like
a bishop!—and surely that's the biggest risk of all! I'm in danger
of being damned if I do and damned if I don't." Yes, it is certainly
possible to see the problem in that way. That is exactly how the
servant in the Gospel *did* see it, and he didn't know which way to
turn: "Lord, I know that you are a hard man . . . and being afraid
I went and hid your talent in the earth" (Mt. 25:24–25, DR). He
made the wrong decision—the fearfully wrong decision. Our Lord,

for our instruction, told him so, saying that he was not only timid or slothful, but wicked! Our Blessed Lord, ever ready to be full of gentleness and compassion, our Blessed Lord in whom beats the Most Sacred Heart of Love, called him wicked, and had him cast out into the exterior darkness!

Isn't that stunning to those of us who habitually think of God as an easy mark? Is not the priesthood of the laity, therefore, as existing in parents, an awesome responsibility? And must we not therefore reform? Must we not hasten to learn how to be little priests in our little churches, and then learn how to exercise our priesthood there? For that we are in need of an inner and an outer preparation. Nearly sixteen years have elapsed since the opening of the Council. What a blessing it would have been for the Church and the entire world if we had all listened to it with the ear of our hearts, if we had all begun, with simplicity, the inner, personal, moral renewal which it called for and which Pope Paul VI ceaselessly urged upon us. So, as we say year after year at the beginning of Lent: "*Now* is the time to rise from sleep!"

The inner preparation now, as always, is a matter of prayer and study. Quite aside from the fact that we owe to God the worship of our prayer, we must pray for two other reasons. First, because we have to learn to love, and, second, because the truths of our faith must become living in our hearts, otherwise, our children will never catch their fire from us.

First, we must learn to love. Indeed, that is why we are gathered here at this National Congress of the Sacred Heart of Jesus, of whom Saint John wrote: "Having loved his own who were in the world, he loved them unto the end" (Jn. 31:1, DR)—to the very extreme and totality of love. And we have to ask ourselves what the connection is between the boundless love of His Heart for us, and our learning to love. Why, in fact, do we, with our hearts of stone, spend energy and time and money coming together to celebrate the fire and tenderness of the Sacred Heart of Jesus? We are here in our poverty, begging to have our cold, hard hearts warmed and softened by His. Somewhere in the Divine Office—I forget where—we read these melting words:

> You must not examine whether your heart is pleasing to Him, but
> whether His Heart is pleasing to you; and looking at His Heart
> is the same as rejoicing in it, for His Heart is so gentle, so sweet,
> so gracious, so much in love with His poor, feeble creatures,
> providing they acknowledge their need: so good to the needy and
> the penitent! And who could fail to love this royal Heart which
> mothers us in such a fatherly way!

Saint John says, as though it were elementary: "We love him
because he first loved us" (see 1 Jn. 4:19). What a humble and
beautiful thought that is, when true. But is it true with us? With the
saints, yes. Saint Hilary said, "I realize indeed, almighty God and
Father, that the overriding duty of my life to you is that you should
be the subject of all my words and all my thoughts" (De Trinitate,
1:37, 38). Saint Paul said, "For me, to live is Christ" (Phil. 1:21,
DR). Saint Augustine cried out in an ecstasy of sorrow and jubila-
tion: "Late have I loved Thee, O Beauty so ancient and so new; late
have I loved Thee!" (Confessions, bk. 10, chap. 27).

Have we such love in our hearts, ready to be conveyed to
our children? If we desire to have it, if we steadily pray to have
it, then, in a measure, we have it, and must thank Him who has
given it; for nothing but that love can make the truths of our faith
become alive in our hearts, so that our children can catch that fire
which Our Lord came to cast upon the earth.

For our inner preparation, we also must know the individual
truths of our holy faith so as to be able to teach them simply
and surely to our children. We parents can bear in mind, for our
comfort, that poor Saint Francis Xavier never had one single
filmstrip, and yet he managed somehow! Our task is smaller.
How vain it is to think about evangelization on a grand scale if
we decline to work first on the tiny field of our own families! To
become a Doctor of Sacred Theology is neither possible nor necessary for most of us, but to want to know our faith and live from
it is both possible and necessary. Again, Pope Paul VI constantly
tried to help us. Ten years ago, he proclaimed his glorious Credo
of the People of God for our sakes. If any Catholic parent says, "Oh
yes, I want to help my children to be good Catholics, but oh no, I

haven't looked at Pope Paul's *Credo*," I would feel fairly safe in saying that that parent is simply not serious. (You will remember that Our Lord used stronger language!)

There must be, then, an outer preparation. What would we think of a missionary priest who set himself up in wild mission territory as pastor, but had no church, no daily schedule, no ritual or program of any kind, simply saying: "Here I am, and there you are; and that makes us a parish!" It may sound a little silly, and it is, but I'm afraid it's what we of the general priesthood do a good deal of the time. We cannot effectively exercise our priesthood in the home, and the home cannot effectively be a little Church without a program, a cult, a "liturgy of the family." And we're sadly behind in this. Therefore, we must all be grateful that a centrally important step has been taken with the beautiful act of the Enthronement in many homes and the beautiful forms in which that act has found expression. As in a Church, so in a home—the first and all-important act is its dedication to the Triune God. That is what we find so beautifully in the consecration of the home to the Sacred Heart of Jesus [see Appendix 1]. For there we find Jesus Himself, and He has said, "He who sees Me sees the Father" (see Jn. 14:19). Likewise, the Sacred Heart discloses to us the love of Jesus, and the love of Jesus is the Holy Spirit. So, in this public acknowledgement of the sovereignty of the Holy Trinity, and in His publicly taking possession of our home, it becomes thereby a House of God, *domus Dei,* "a little Church." And wherever Jesus has His dwelling—whether in Nazareth or in Heaven—there, according to His will, His Holy Mother also dwells—enthroned above all other creatures.

In any inclusive "liturgy of the family" there must also be a public and ever-renewed acknowledgement that, as a little church, the home is specifically a localization of the universal Church. We go to God, and God comes to us, in and through His Church. This should be signified, perhaps, by a showing of the papal colors, or a noble representation of Saint Peter's Basilica.

These things, together with the enthroned Sacred Heart, point to the need in each home for some space which is at once part of the habitation and yet somewhat set apart—as is inherent in the very meaning of the word *ecclesia*. It is true that the whole dwelling and all its life is placed under the sign of the Heart of Christ the King, but, at the same time, it is fitting that one area be set apart exclusively for His Glory. This area, whether it be a room or merely a corner or an area in a passageway, should, at all times, be tended with special care and, as far as possible, be a little space of silence; for in these days, silence is the most unusual thing of all, and is capable of drawing our awakened attention to what is there.

With this, we have our domestic Church built and blessed. What comes next? Well, we have heard that the father occupies in the home the place of God, the place of a Vicar of Christ, the place of a bishop, the place of a priest. That's quite a place! It ought to be made ready, be liturgically established, and be given a sacramental dimension. In some mode the father should be consecrated and installed in his tiny see, while the general priesthood of the mother and of all the baptized within the household is also recognized, declared, and honored.

This development, too, is foreshadowed at the end of the rite of the Enthronement, with the optional "Parental Blessing." But the very imparting of a blessing is a priestly act, and what I am here urging is a rite expressing the fact that the parents of a family do have a priestly character which enables them to perform a priestly act. We're rather far from that at present, as far as I have discovered. In my copy of the Church's Ritual, dated 1964, we find a great diversity of blessings. There is a blessing of children . . . of mothers . . . of a bonfire . . . of bees and goats and silkworms and pigs. It is a long, beautiful, truly Catholic list of blessable subjects. There is even something triumphantly described as a deprecatory blessing against pests! BUT—of fathers? Nothing! Of the heads of families? No mention! Of the bishop of the domestic Church? Not a word! That's bad! Someone will have to appoint a Committee, because it would certainly help us to remember our priestly dignity—and to grow into it—if there were a liturgical, formal recognition of it.

With that, we would then have the domestic Church and its priest—still in wild mission territory! Now what? What will be its content, its ritual, its life? What will be the daily round of prayer, study, and action? It is a large question, with many wrong answers, but also, undoubtedly, some right ones. It will have to be the engrossing topic of another engrossing talk which I shall contrive to give somewhere in the distant future. Suffice it to say here that the form of the family prayer should have in it one role played exclusively by the father or his delegate. Children should be encouraged to take part to the fullest extent of their capabilities, but not beyond that extent, while great care is taken to instill the truth that special participation is a privilege and an honor, to be undertaken in a spirit of deepest reverence, and not as an adventure in the limelight.

Finally, now that the little church is established, its pastor installed, and its worship arranged, the school must be organized, because the parents have been assigned the mission, as we have seen, to be apostles to their children, and must strive to be like the Apostles, like Saint Andrew, for instance. Concerning Saint Andrew's haste to tell Simon, "We have found the Messiah," Saint John Chrysostom said, "Andrew's words are those of one waiting for the Messiah to come from heaven, full of joy that he has come, and hurrying to tell the great news to others" (Homily 19 on the Gospel of John).

Oh, let us hurry to tell our children the great news of our rescue by Jesus Christ crucified, who paid for us the entire contents of His pierced Heart! Let us make haste in fear and love! Through the mouth of the prophet Amos we have heard the foreboding words:

> "Behold, the days are coming," says the Lord GOD, "when I will send a famine on the land; not a famine of bread, nor a thirst for water, but of hearing the words of the LORD. They shall wander from sea to sea, and from north to east: they shall run to and fro, to seek the word of the LORD, but they shall not find it. In that day the fair virgins and the young men shall faint for thirst." (Amos 8:11–13, RSVCE)

It is not said that the Word does not exist, but that it is not given to them! And who will receive the blame? They especially will be blamed whose special and immediate task it was to nourish the children with the Word of Life: the parents who have been given their share in "the priestly, prophetic and royal office of Christ and therefore have their own share in the mission of the whole people of God in the Church and in the world,"[5] and first of all and above all in the sanctuary of the domestic Church, their families.

Our blessed Lord warned that "he that shall scandalize one of these little ones that believe in me, it were better for him that a millstone should be hanged about his neck, and that he should be drowned in the depth of the sea" (Mt. 18:6, DR). And a scandal it is indeed that, in many, many instances, the doors of our little domestic churches are closed against the entry of Jesus Christ. Within them, no songs of praise and thanks and love rise up to the throne of grace; no space is set apart for silence and prayer; no period of time each day is set aside and totally given to Him who made us and from whom comes every good and perfect gift. A Church with an absentee priest, and no horarium,[6] no lights, no incense, no flowers, no singing, no hearing of the word of God—what is that but a dead and joyless Church? Who will bring it back to life and joy?

God, Thou wilt turn and breathe life into us again; then will Thy people find their joy in Thee! *Deus, to conversus vivificabis nos, et plebs tua laetabitur in te!*

---

[5] Second Vatican Council, Decree on the Apostolate of the Laity *Apostolicam Actuositatem* (November 11, 1965), chap. 1, no. 2.

[6] Schedule of prayer

CHAPTER VII

Let There Be Light!

LEON AND MAUREEN SUPRENANT

Leon likes to note that as the youngest of fourteen children he has much to be grateful for, including the fact that his parents didn't have the good sense to stop at thirteen!

Yet, even though we were both raised in large, Catholic families and had the advantage of a Catholic school education, we left the Church in our youth and didn't come back until we were in our twenties. Our newly rediscovered love for Christ not only led us to study His teaching, but also to take a fresh look at traditional prayers and devotions used by Christian disciples for countless generations as aids to growth in the spiritual life.

And so we enthusiastically embraced the Rosary as the most time-tested and efficacious spiritual weapon in our arsenal after the sacred liturgy itself. For Leon, it was a case of remembering something that was deeply embedded in his heart, as though his conversion also healed his spiritual amnesia. For Maureen, there was the intense realization that the many Rosaries offered by her pious grandmother played a vital role in her radical acceptance of God's love and healing in her life.

Even so, as we began praying the Rosary in earnest in the 1980s, it always seemed strange to us that we had an entire set of mysteries for Luke 1–2, namely, the Joyful Mysteries, and then we had to jump to Luke 22 for the Agony in the Garden, the First Sorrowful Mystery. It seemed to us that Luke 3, Luke 4, Luke 5, and so on, up to Luke 22, also contained much solid meat for contemplation. The Rosary has always been considered a "compendium of the Gospel," but it seemed that some of the pages were missing.

Therefore, we welcomed Pope John Paul II's introduction of the Luminous Mysteries as a means of encouraging the faithful to prayerfully contemplate Christ's public ministry. The Holy Father did this in his 2002 apostolic letter *Rosarium Virginis Mariae* ("The Rosary of the Virgin Mary"),[1] at the start of the 25th year of his remarkable pontificate.

Even more, we're excited that so many people, young and old, have taken advantage of this teaching and the 2002–03 "Year of the Rosary" as a means of redirecting our gaze upon the face of Christ, the one Savior of the world, through the heart of the Blessed Virgin Mary. Further, while everyone can benefit from the devout recitation of the Rosary, the devotion is particularly suited to the renewal of marriage and family life, as we strive to make our homes "schools of prayer" that give honor to our Triune God.

Most of us learned in school that "all roads lead to Rome" (or perhaps away from Rome, depending on one's perspective). Of course, we were talking about Rome's elaborate transportation system. Yet, "all roads lead to Rome" is also true in the sense that all glimmers or bits of truth find their fulfillment in Christ and His Church. Ultimately, all roads lead to Christ, the one Savior of the world, or away from Him.

Focusing on the goal of union with Christ is essential for understanding the value of the new Luminous Mysteries, or "Mysteries of Light." Pope John Paul II emphasized that the Rosary is not an end in itself, but a means to three inter-related ends: (1) personal

---

[1] This apostolic letter is available online at www.vatican.va/holy_father/john_paul_ii/ apost_letters/ documents/ hf_jp-ii_apl_20021016_rosarium-virginis-mariae_en.html.

contemplation, as we gaze with Mary upon the face of Christ; (2) the formation of the People of God, as we unite ourselves to the Church; and (3) the new evangelization, as the Rosary provides the spiritual foundation for bringing the Gospel to our contemporaries, just as it did for Saint Dominic and his spiritual progeny.

We've heard a few people complain about the new mysteries. They liked the Rosary as it was and experience the new mysteries as some sort of undesirable novelty.

The situation may be likened to that of a commuter who's accustomed to taking the same road to work each day. The governor, at no taxpayer's expense, constructs an alternate route, which can be just as fast and pleasant of a drive. If there's an accident, a traffic jam, or construction on one route, the commuter can take the other route. Who would complain about that?

Similarly, the faithful are completely free to pray the Rosary as they always have. It's just that now we have another means of entering into the mystery of Christ. In addition to introducing the new mysteries, *Rosarium Virginis Mariae* provides ample practical guidance for praying the Rosary well. The Pope's goal was not to encumber or frustrate the faithful, but to help us pray better, to help us contemplate the face of Christ.

Love for the Church

One of the prayers that is sometimes added at the end of the Rosary asks the Lord to grant us the grace through our meditation of the mysteries of the Rosary to "imitate what they contain and obtain what they promise." Each of the five "mysteries" or events in Jesus' public life that comprise the Luminous Mysteries provides much food for contemplation. We recommend good meditation guides and reflections on these mysteries to help plumb their depths.[2] Here we want to mention two refrains that run through all the Luminous Mysteries, which we think are especially important for families.

---

[2] We especially recommend Tim Gray, *Luminous Mysteries* (Steubenville, OH: Emmaus Road Publishing, 2005).

The first refrain is "love for the Church." We live at a time when many people are to some extent open to Jesus Christ, but want nothing to do with His Church. So what has the Pope done? He has encouraged us, by means of the Luminous Mysteries, to contemplate the public ministry of Christ. What was at the heart of His public ministry? Nothing other than the proclamation of the Kingdom of God—that it was "at hand." Well, was it or not? About a century ago, French heretic Alfred Loisy bemoaned that Christ promised a Kingdom, but all that we got was the Church.

We joyfully respond that the Church is, in fact, the Kingdom of God on earth. The Church continues, despite our own human failings and weaknesses, to bring the light of Christ to all the world. It's no accident that the central document issued by the Second Vatican Council (1962–65) on the mystery of the Church is called *Lumen Gentium*, or "Light of the Nations."

The fifth and culminating Luminous Mystery is the Institution of the Eucharist. Pope John Paul II began his final encyclical letter by stating that "the Church draws her life from the Eucharist."[3] Similarly, the Catechism says that the Eucharist "makes the Church" (no. 1396). In other words, the Eucharist is the most tangible and profound manner in which Christ keeps His promise to remain with His Church to the end, that He will never abandon us. It's God's way of making present and effective in our lives the saving effects of Christ's sacrifice on the Cross. It's God's way of continuing to be Emmanuel, or "God-with-us," through His ongoing real presence in the Eucharist. And it's God's way of uniting us in His family, the Church.

Interestingly, the disciples on the road to Emmaus, as far as we know, were the first lay people to attend "Mass." What did their Eucharistic experience lead them to do? They went back to Jerusalem, to the company of the apostles. In other words, it drew them back into the heart of the Church (see Lk. 24:13–35).

---

[3] Pope John Paul II, encyclical letter On the Eucharist in Its Relationship to the Church *Ecclesia de Eucharistia* (April 17, 2003), no. 1, accessible at www.vatican.va/ holy_father/special_features/encyclicals/documents/hf_jp-ii_enc_20030417_ecclesia_eucharistia_en.html.

Families need to love the Church as our Mother (cf. CCC 169 and 507), as our true home in the family of God, and not as a merely human institution or outside force that's imposing arbitrary rules on us. Now more than ever, especially given the horrible scandals that have afflicted the Church in our midst, we need to affirm—to proclaim from the rooftops—our love for the Church!

Do Whatever He Tells You

The other refrain running through the Luminous Mysteries is the virtue of obedience. Of the new mysteries, the one that we gravitate toward is the Wedding at Cana, and not just because of its obvious connection to the Sacrament of Marriage. Mary's simple words at Cana are striking and still ring out today: "Do whatever Jesus tells you" (cf. Jn. 2:5). This message calls forth our obedience. In imitation of the Blessed Virgin Mary, we are called to hear the word of God, ponder it in our hearts, and then do it.

This theme runs through the other Luminous Mysteries as well. For example, in the Transfiguration, our heavenly Father declares, "This is my beloved son . . . listen to him" (Mt. 17:5). Even in the Institution of the Eucharist, the Church is commanded to "do this in memory of me" (Lk. 22:19). In fact, Jesus bluntly tells us that if we don't "do this," we have no life in us (cf. Jn. 6:53). So the stakes are high. The entire proclamation of the Kingdom calls forth from us the "obedience of faith" (Rom. 1:5). In short, we need to do what Jesus tells us.

Perhaps it would be easier if Jesus were standing in our midst telling us what to do. And yet, even though He no longer walks the earth, He does speak to us through His Church, most notably through the successors of Saint Peter and the other apostles. Jesus says if we hear and obey them, we hear and obey Him (cf. Lk. 10:16). Furthermore, if we hear and obey Our Lord, then we are also obeying Our Blessed Mother, who lovingly exhorts us to do whatever He tells us. Not surprisingly, then, the Book of Revelation describes the woman's (i.e., the Blessed Virgin Mary's) offspring as "those who keep the commandments of God and bear testimony to Jesus" (Rev. 12:17).

Our oldest daughter's favorite verse (at least she quotes it all the time for Leon's benefit) is Colossians 3:21: "Fathers, do not provoke your children, lest they become discouraged." Fair enough. Leon will be judged on this verse and similar verses, as will priests and bishops—our spiritual fathers. We've encountered many Catholics who are angry, provoked, or discouraged, and those who so alienate the faithful will be held strictly accountable by the Lord.

But Leon is still ready for our daughter when she playfully cites her verse, as he counters with the preceding verse: "Children, obey your parents in everything, for this pleases the Lord." Those in authority will be judged on how they exercise their authority. We, on the other hand, will be judged according to how we obey legitimate authority.

There's the story of Saint Margaret Mary, who once refused the wimpy penance given to her by her confessor. Instead, she offered more extreme sacrifices of her own choosing. Our Lord appeared to her and gently rebuked her, reminding her that obedience is more important than her heroic sacrifices. As the psalmist writes, "sacrifice and offering you do not want, but ears open to obedience you gave me" (Ps. 40:7 NAB).

Only God's authority is limitless. Surely we're not bound to follow laws or directives that are immoral or which go beyond the scope of one's authority. But in general, our disposition toward Church authority should be one of respectful obedience—an obedience that is neither naively blind nor cynically distrustful. As Christian parents, we must encourage our children to do whatever Jesus tells them and to hear the Good Shepherd's voice coming from His Church.

Focus on the Family

In *Rosarium Virginis Mariae*, Pope John Paul II identified two compelling reasons as to why the revival of the Rosary in our time is an urgent priority. First, he noted our desperate need for the gift of peace, specifically citing the 9/11 attacks and the escalating violence and bloodshed throughout the world. Only

Christ, the Prince of Peace, is able to break down the barriers of hostility that divide peoples and nations (cf. Eph. 2:14).

We tend to forget about the spiritual dimension of conflict when it's right in front of us. Our response when war breaks out is to spend hours in front of CNN or Fox News, not the Blessed Sacrament, calling upon "embedded" journalists, not guardian angels. And so the Pope gave us a timely reminder that when we enter into the Rosary, we can't help but be caught up in the quest for peace. Without getting into a scholarly discussion of "just war" principles and related issues, the Holy Father emphasized that prayer—and specifically the Rosary—is the most effective weapon we have against the discord and disorder within ourselves, within our families, and within our troubled world.

Pope John Paul II offered a second reason for renewed attention to the Rosary. He saw the Rosary as a means of building up the family. He frequently emphasized that as the family goes, so goes the Church and society, because the family is "the first and vital cell of society."[4]

As vital cells of the universal Church, each Christian family as a "domestic Church" or "church in miniature" contributes to the overall well-being of the Body of Christ. Healthy families can be a source of healing, growth, and vitality. The widespread breakdown of the family, however, is a cancer that afflicts the Church and stunts her growth.

In this context, the Holy Father reminds us of the critical importance of family prayer. Surely this is not to the detriment of personal prayer, prayer of married couples, and liturgical prayer. But we must understand and take to heart the adage that "the family that prays together stays together." This adage may sound negative or at least defensive at first. Surely families today are menaced by forces of disintegration that threaten to tear us apart from God and from one another, and family prayer is understandably a

---

[4] Pope John Paul II, apostolic exhortation On the Christian Family in the Modern World *Familiaris Consortio* (November 21, 1981), no. 42, quoting Vatican II, *Decree on the Apostolate of the Laity*, no. 11. In this apostolic exhortation, the Holy Father emphasized that "the future of humanity passes by way of the family" (no. 86).

response to such a threat. But even more, family prayer helps us to play "offense" by fostering strong, intact families that can serve as "spiritual powerhouses" in the Kingdom of God.

From our own experience, we readily admit that all this is easier said than done. Family prayer is very challenging, as many families are often too busy to communicate with one another, let alone to come together to communicate with God. We can also very easily get caught up with the wrong sorts of images and values, especially through excessive recourse to television and the Internet.

Several important things go on at the same time while we pray the Rosary. First, there are the prayers themselves, which have a calming effect and dispose us to communion with God. Second, there is the contemplation of the mystery from the life of Christ. But the family Rosary goes even further. As we strive to pray in communion with Christ through the heart of Mary, we remember the mystery and it becomes present and effective in our lives and gets woven into the very fabric of our lives. Our family's joys get woven into the Joyful Mysteries, our family's sufferings and difficulties get woven into the Sorrowful Mysteries. As Pope John Paul II noted:

> Our heart can embrace in the decades of the Rosary all the events that make up the lives of individuals, families, nations, the Church, and all mankind. Our personal concerns and those of our neighbor, especially those who are closest to us, who are dearest to us. Thus the simple prayer of the Rosary marks the rhythm of human life.[5]

We have found that praying the Rosary as a family at the end of the day adds an element of recollection into the hubbub of our household. The rhythm of the prayer has a remarkably calming effect on the rhythm of our family's life.

We know a family in which the father, every evening at a set time, tells the kids to get their weapons. That means it's time for the Rosary. Surely the Rosary is a weapon for our own individual

---

[5] Pope John Paul II, apostolic letter *Rosarium Virginis Mariae* (October 16, 2002), no. 2, quoting Angelus: *Insegnamenti di Giovanni Paolo II*, I (1978), 75–76.

spiritual battles, but it's also a weapon for the family's spiritual battles. Sometimes these are actual battles as well, as on occasion this "meditative prayer" is anything but meditative when the kids are screaming or wrestling over prayer books or getting into something. Sometimes that's part of the battle.

Saint Matthew says in his Gospel that no one knows the Father except the Son and those to whom the Son reveals Him (see Mt. 11:25–27). He also records Saint Peter's confession of faith, to which Our Lord responds that flesh and blood have not revealed this to him, but rather that this was a gift from His Father in heaven (see Mt. 16:17).

In order to contemplate the face of Christ, we too need a revelation from above. If we're honest, we must humbly admit that we don't know how to pray as we ought even in the best of conditions, though we do need to do what we reasonably can to create an environment in our homes that's conducive to prayer. We know that Our Lord showers with grace those families who hang in there when praying the Rosary with their rambunctious children, as the occasional or not-so-occasional distractions of normal family life become incorporated into the rhythm of the family's prayer.

Let the Children Come

One of our favorite verses is Matthew 19:14, in which Jesus says, "Let the children come to me, and do not hinder them; for to such belongs the kingdom of heaven." This verse really connects with our mission as a married couple to teach our children "to pray and discern their vocations as children of God," beginning in our children's "earliest years" (CCC 2226).

The Rosary is a simple yet profound prayer, capable of engaging young and old alike. By way of illustration, once a young man entered a train and sat down across from an elderly man who was praying the Rosary. They struck up a conversation, and the young man explained that he didn't need superstitious practices like the Rosary, because he was going to be a scientist. The elderly man looked up, puzzled and somewhat hurt.

Eventually, the young man's stop came up, so he asked for the elderly man's card so he could tell him more about science. The next day, the young scientist pulled out the card, ready to further educate the old man. The card read, "Louis Pasteur, Professor and Dean of Faculty of Sciences, University of Paris."

While brilliant men like Louis Pasteur have found inexhaustible riches in the Rosary, the prayer is not beyond the smallest children, who are naturally drawn to the rhythmic repetition of the prayers—not to mention the Rosary beads! The Rosary gets children involved, too. Our children frequently lead the different mysteries, which at times can make for some unusual Rosaries, especially when the children are not quite old enough to count or remember all the prayers.

Further, the Rosary encourages children to think outside themselves as we recall the many prayer intentions that have been entrusted to our family. Children have very good memories, and they tend to remember and bring up during family prayer many people and situations that we might otherwise have forgotten about.

In order to develop the contemplative aspect of the prayer, we have found it helpful to have picture books and sacred images for the younger children to look at during the prayer time. As they get older, we look for prayer books with a little more text. We're blessed in that our parish church has fifteen of the mysteries of the Rosary depicted in magnificent stained glass windows. These are Gospels that little kids (and adults!) can read. It's amazing how much gets soaked in through their consideration of the mysteries. This practice builds their religious imagination, too. Once one of our daughters told us that the Coronation of Mary (fifth Glorious Mystery) was her favorite mystery. This seemed odd in a sense, because the Coronation can be a little more difficult for even some adults. When asked why it was her favorite, she said, "Because when we pray this mystery, I think about what heaven must be like."

The Rosary also provides a magnificent opportunity for biblical formation and family catechesis. The Popes have emphasized that the Rosary must not degenerate into a mere rattling of prayers. We noticed this once with one of our sons, who for a time prayed, "lead us *now* into temptation." Unfortunately, it seemed that Our Lord was answering this wayward prayer! That's why it's so important to announce each mystery, perhaps adding a short biblical reading that draws everyone into the mystery. Pope John Paul II in *Rosarium Virginis Mariae* said that the group recitation of the Rosary presents "a significant catechetical opportunity."[6] This is especially the case when the Rosary is prayed with children.

The family Rosary fosters engaging, impromptu discussions. For instance, when praying the Joyful Mysteries during Advent and the Christmas season, the children connect the mysteries with Old Testament prophecies concerning the Messiah. They ask very good questions about how the Epiphany and the Flight into Egypt fit chronologically with the Presentation in the Temple. Sometimes, they ask questions that make us do a little homework, such as the time one daughter asked how the apostles present at the Transfiguration knew that the two people with Our Lord were Moses and Elijah.

We try to see the Rosary and indeed all family prayer as an integral part of the daily rhythm of our lives, along with chores, schoolwork, reading, and other activities. It's not something to "squeeze in," and it decidedly is not something foreign to or disconnected from the rest of our family time. In this regard, we place special emphasis on the family dinner, which is a cherished time in which we pray together, eat together, and enjoy one another's company on a daily basis. One thing we do is go around the table thanking the Lord for a blessing received that day. It's one small way that we try to foster in all of us, including the youngest children, a spirit of prayer and gratitude.

When it comes to incorporating the Rosary or other pious devotions or practices into the family's routine, we think of Leon's battle through the years with his weight. He has been on many diets, and has lost hundreds of pounds. However, when those

---

[6] Pope John Paul II, *Rosarium Virginis Mariae*, no 17.

diets haven't brought about a sustainable change in lifestyle, the weight inevitably comes back when the enthusiasm dies down. So rather than make unreasonable, unsustainable goals, we recommend gradually incorporating practices that become second nature for the family. It's often said that the Church moves in centuries. Well, we can pray in decades—perhaps praying a decade of the Rosary while making a short trip to the store or waiting at the doctor's office. What's important is that we take advantage of opportunities in the present moment, so that not only our bodies, but also, in a real sense, our homes may be temples of the Holy Spirit.

Discussion Questions

1. Does my family pray the Rosary? What is my family's attitude toward the Rosary?

2. What Mystery(ies) of the Rosary do I find easiest to pray? What Mystery(ies) are the most challenging? Why?

3. Do I love the Church? Do I manifest this attitude in my words and actions? What can I do proactively to foster a love for the Church in my children and other loved ones?

4. Do I really recognize that all authority comes from God? How is authority exercised in my family? Do I joyfully obey those who have authority over me?

5. Do I use my time well? Do I use leisure time for prayer or other spiritual pursuits? Does my family make time for God and one another?

Leon and Maureen Suprenant have six children and one grandchild, and live in Steubenville, Ohio. Leon is the president of Catholics United for the Faith, while Maureen homeschools the children and makes a very busy house a home.

CHAPTER VIII

The Bride
God's People Restored

STEPHEN AND RACHEL PIMENTEL

Throughout Holy Scripture, one of the most prominent images for the people of God is that of the bride. This image rests on an analogy between the two types of covenants most important in the life of Israel: the covenant that unites man and woman in marriage, and the covenant that unites God and the people He has chosen and redeemed. In the Israelite understanding, a covenant between parties joins them in a familial union and calls them to faithfulness toward each other. Hence, it was natural that human marriage and divine election, which share these covenantal features, would be brought into correspondence with each other.

This correspondence was first described by the Old Testament prophets, for whom human marriage served as a type of the union between God and His people, a union that was ultimately to be achieved by the Messiah. The development of this prophetic typology culminates in the Song of Songs, interpreted according to its allegorical sense. In the Gospels, the Messianic significance of the typology is brought to the forefront, as Jesus describes Himself as the divine Bridegroom at His wedding

feast. Saint Paul illuminates the significance of the correspondence of covenants for human marriage by using the union of
Christ and the Church to explain the respective calling and
duties of spouses.

Marital Difficulties

If Israel's covenant with God is like a marriage, then her
worship of other gods is analogous to adultery. In the oracles of
Hosea, such adultery becomes a vivid symbol for idolatry. God
used the unhappy course of Hosea's marriage to Gomer as a
prophetic symbol to depict the northern kingdom of Israel as an
unfaithful wife and, indeed, a harlot. Just as Gomer sold herself
as a harlot, so Israel sold herself to the gods of Canaan and
Assyria. Thus, in the prophecy of Hosea, the adulterous harlotry
of Gomer becomes a shocking depiction of Israel's idolatrous
participation in pagan cults (cf. Hos. 2:4-8; 8:9).

However, Hosea's marriage to Gomer serves not only to
condemn Israel but, more generally, to characterize God's
covenant with Israel. God weds Israel and requires of her the
covenantal virtues of charity (*hesed*) and knowledge (*da'at*), the
essential elements of conjugal union (cf. Hos. 6:6). However,
Israel did not live out these covenantal virtues but, instead,
acted unfaithfully by worshipping other gods. Therefore, she
would be punished and taken into the wilderness (cf. Hos.
2:9–14). Nevertheless, God will remain faithful to her. Just
as Hosea forgives Gomer, so God will forgive Israel. Indeed,
Hosea foretells a day when God will bring Israel into a New
Covenant of charity (cf. Hos. 2:15–19) and make of her a faithful bride (cf. Hos. 2:20).

Jerusalem, Old and New

Isaiah continues the use of marriage as a type of the covenant between God and His people but applies it to the southern
kingdom of Judah and, in particular, to the city of Jerusalem. In
Isaiah's prophetic understanding, there are only two possibili-
ties open to Jerusalem: she can fulfill her calling as the city of

God and become the fruitful bride of God and mother to her people, or she can emulate the city of man and become a barren harlot. All who repent of idolatry and turn to God, whether of the remnant of Israel or faithful Gentiles, become identified with the bride.

The Book of Isaiah begins by charging that Jerusalem has lapsed from faithfulness to become a harlot (cf. Is. 1:21) and will therefore undergo a period of punishment. Yet, God will not allow Jerusalem to remain forsaken forever. By the end of the book, Isaiah proclaims that the shame of her youth will be forgotten, and God the Creator will again be her husband and Redeemer (cf. Is. 54:4–8). Jerusalem will be given a "new name" (Is. 62:1–2) and become a perfect bride over whom God rejoices (cf. Is. 62:3–5). However, the New Jerusalem will not consist merely of a restoration of the city's former temporal status. Rather, God Himself will "create Jerusalem" anew within a "new heavens and a new earth" in which "the former things shall not be remembered" (Is. 65:17–18). In Isaiah's culminating vision, this New Jerusalem gives birth to a people "in one moment" (Is. 66:7–8).

Jeremiah brings together Hosea's prophecy against Israel and Isaiah's prophecy against Judah, explaining that the fates of the two kingdoms are intertwined. Although Israel was the wife of God, she became an adulterous harlot and suffered the punishment of exile (cf. Jer. 3:6–8). "Yet her false sister Judah did not fear, but she too went and played the harlot," worshipping idols and thus "committing adultery with stone and tree" (Jer. 3:8–9). As a result, Judah will follow Israel into exile. Yet, Jeremiah foretells a day when both Israel and Judah will return from exile (cf. Jer. 31:21–28) and be restored to God in a New Covenant (cf. Jer. 31:31–35). Jeremiah's prophecy promises great spiritual blessings to those who repent of idolatry and enter the New Covenant. God will write His law "upon their hearts" and give them covenantal knowledge of Himself, "from the least of them to the greatest" (Jer. 31:33–34).

Seeking the Bridegroom

The Song of Songs presents the highest development within the Old Testament of the theme of God's marriage to His people. In its literal sense, the Song of Songs describes the love of a bridegroom and bride around the time of their wedding. In addition to its literal sense, Catholic tradition since Origen has consistently interpreted the Song in the allegorical sense.[1]

In general, the allegorical sense of Scripture relates events to their significance for faith in Christ. According to its allegorical sense, the Song describes the covenantal relation of love between God and His people. When this allegorical sense is explored, the Song reveals the dynamic structure of this covenantal relation. The essential dynamic begins in the situation of Israel's separation from God. Israel searches for God but is unable to find Him on her own. God periodically visits His people in order to prepare and purify them, but then withdraws, initiating another period of searching.

The Song opens with the bride declaring her desire for intimacy with the Bridegroom (cf. Song 1:2). However, this desire cannot be satisfied at once. For a long time, the bride "must be content with the friends of the Bridegroom," the prophets of the Old Testament.[2] The bride asks the Bridegroom to "draw me after you" (Song 1:4) and so end her exile. The Bridegroom Himself is "the king" (Song 1:4), representing the Davidic Messiah. The bride immediately begins her search for the Bridegroom (cf. Song 1:5–2:7). She is rewarded with a visitation of the Bridegroom (cf. Song 2:8–17), after which He departs. The bride is distressed by her separation from the Bridegroom and sets out at night to seek Him (cf. Song 3:1–5). On a second occasion, the Bridegroom visits the bride (cf. Song 5:2), but she is not ready to receive Him (cf. Song 5:3–5),

---

[1] On the distinct senses of Scripture, see CCC 116–117. For Origen's foundational commentary on the Song, see R. P. Lawson, ed. *Origen: The Song of Songs Commentary and Homilies*, ed. Johannes Quasten and Joseph C. Plumpe, *Ancient Christian Writers: The Works of the Fathers in Translation*, vol. 26 (Westminster, MD: The Newman Press, 1957).
[2] Lawson, *Origen*, 11.

and so He departs (cf. Song 5:6). She again searches for Him through the streets of the city at night, and is taken for a harlot by the watchmen and is beaten (cf. Song 5:7).

There is, then, a movement within the Song of Songs from the Davidic toward the New Covenant, a movement representing the incremental purification and restoration of the people of God. The Song reaches its culmination with its description of covenantal love as a "seal" upon the "heart" (Song 8:6), corresponding to the New Covenant law of love (cf. Jer. 31:33; Gal. 5:14). This love is so powerful as to rival even death: "for love is strong as death, jealousy is cruel as the grave" (Song 8:6). In the New Covenant, the Messiah will finally wed His bride, at last purified and restored. The Song of Songs can be read as a series of hymns for this wedding.

The Wedding of the Son

In the New Testament, the Bridegroom is explicitly identified as the Messiah. At the start of Jesus' public ministry, John the Baptist describes himself as the "friend of the bridegroom," who rejoices in the advent of the Bridegroom among His people (Jn. 3:29). Jesus describes His ministry as bestowing the presence of the Bridegroom among His disciples (cf. Mt. 9:15; Mk. 2:19–20; Lk. 5:34–35).

During His last sojourn in Jerusalem at the end of His earthly ministry, Jesus related the parable of the marriage feast given for the son of a king (cf. Mt. 22:1–10), which depicts the impending rejection of His ministry and its aftermath. (In the parable, the son represents Jesus, the Bridegroom, and the king represents God the Father.[3]) The guests initially invited to the wedding, representing the leaders of Jerusalem, contemptuously refused to attend and even murdered the king's servants. As Isaiah foresaw, Jerusalem had chosen to reject God's calling and emulate the city of man. However, the wedding was not cancelled or even

---

[3] The parable follows the marital typology from earlier in the Gospel in that the son, representing Jesus, is the one to be married.

delayed. Instead, the king sent troops and "burned their city" (Mt. 22:7).[4] He then sent his servants "to the thoroughfares" with a new round of invitations, and "the wedding hall was filled with guests," the new disciples of Jesus (Mt. 22:9–10). Thus, the parable of the wedding of the son outlines the course of the purification and restoration of the people of God in the first century. Another closely related use of the wedding feast symbolism occurs in Revelation 19–21, as discussed below.

The Bridegroom's Gift

In the Epistle to the Ephesians, Saint Paul applies the mystery of Christ to the family, understood as the domestic Church, beginning with the unity between husband and wife (cf. Eph. 5:21–6:9). Saint Paul's profound analysis of the relation of husband and wife reveals that the covenantal understanding of marriage is not merely a metaphor, but an integral part of God's plan for mankind. As Pope John Paul II explains, in "the sacrifice which Jesus Christ makes of Himself on the Cross for His Bride, the Church . . . there is entirely revealed that plan which God has imprinted on the humanity of man and woman since their creation." (FC, no. 13)

The starting point of Saint Paul's reflection in Ephesians is the mystery of Christ, who "gave himself up" for the Church on the Cross and continues to do so in the Eucharist (Eph. 5:25; cf. Lk. 22:19–20). The Eucharist is the sacramental renewal of the covenant by which Christ makes Himself present within the Church and gives her true knowledge of Him. "The renewal in the Eucharist of the covenant between the Lord and man draws the faithful into the compelling love of Christ and sets them on fire."[5] As Christ gives Himself to the Church in the Eucharist, so the husband should give himself to his wife in marriage (cf. Eph. 5:25). Indeed, the husband's love for his wife is a participation in Christ's love for the Church.

---

[4] This prediction of the destruction of Jerusalem, which took place in AD 70, is consistent with that of the Olivet Discourse. See Lk. 21:20–21.

[5] Second Vatican Council, Constitution on the Sacred Liturgy *Sacrosanctum Concilium*, (December 4, 1963), no. 10.

The Great Mystery

Saint Paul indicates that Adam's marriage to Eve in Gen. 2:20–24 is a type of Christ's union with the Church as His mystical body (cf. Eph. 5:28–31).[6] In the divine economy, Christ brings salvation to the world, not by an extrinsic decree, but through His bodily union with the Church (CCC 772). Through this union, Christ acts as the new Adam to draw the bride into the presence and knowledge of the Father (cf. Jn. 14:6; Mt. 11:27) and so recapitulate all things (cf. Eph. 1:9–10). Hence, the union of Christ and the Church is indeed a "great mystery," whose image is reflected in the relation between husband and wife (cf. Eph. 5:32). Marriage between the baptized is not merely a natural symbol of the union of Christ and the Church. Rather, such marriage is sacramental, entailing a real supernatural participation in the great mystery of that union.[7] Sacramental marriage is, therefore, an essential part of the economy by which Christ builds up the Church, His bride, until she reaches perfection. This sacramentality entails the indissolubility to which the baptized spouses freely pledge themselves, ratifying their union by a sacred oath or *sacramentum*.[8] In their wedding, they publicly exchange such oaths, grounding their marriage "in the conjugal covenant of irrevocable personal consent" (GS, no. 48).

Sacramentality also reveals the full spiritual meaning of procreation. In the New Covenant, the Church is united to Christ as His mystical body, and the many are joined in that body through Baptism and the Eucharist. In this way, the union of Christ and the Church gives birth to new children of God. In the language of Saint Peter, Christ begets these new children through the seed of the Word (cf. 1 Pet. 1:23). The Church conceives this new life, brings it to fruition, and educates her children to maturity. Christ, as the new Adam and covenantal head of mankind, bestows the

---

[6] Matthias Joseph Scheeben, *The Mysteries of Christianity*, trans. Cyril Vollert, S.J. (Saint Louis; London: B. Herder Book Co., 1946), 374.
[7] Scheeben, *The Mysteries of Christianity*, 601–602.
[8] Ibid., 598.

power of procreation on the members of His body in order to
extend His kingdom. In procreation, the marriage of the baptized
spouses both mirrors and extends the union of Christ and the
Church.[9] Hence, the covenantal communion of bridegroom and
bride, in its spiritual depths, is ordered essentially to procreation.
Procreation is not merely a natural end of marriage but a spiritual
work dedicated to extending the kingdom of God. In a sacramental marriage, the members of Christ's body enter a union ordered
to the extension of that body.[10]

The Bride Unveiled

The Book of Revelation presents the summation of covenantal history as conveyed in Holy Scripture, and, at the climax
of Revelation, is the final appearance of the bride. Revelation
uses symbolic apocalyptic language to convey the theological
significance of the pivotal historical events of the first century
involved in the transition from the Mosaic Covenant to the New
Covenant. These events culminate in the destruction of Jerusalem
in AD 70, as depicted in Revelation 19.

Saint John hears the saints in heaven, the Church Triumphant,
declaring that God "has judged the great harlot," using Isaiah's
description of Jerusalem in rebellion (Rev. 19:1–2). The Church
Triumphant is made up of both Israelites, represented by the
"twenty-four elders" (Rev. 19:4), and Gentiles, represented by
the "great multitude" whose voice is "like the sound of many
waters" (Rev. 19:6). The saints are preparing to rejoice for one
central reason. "The marriage of the Lamb has come, and his
Bride has made herself ready; it was granted her to be clothed
with fine linen, bright and pure" (Rev. 19:7–8). Saint John
immediately notes that "the fine linen" clothing the bride "is
the righteous deeds of the saints" (Rev. 19:8). The angel guiding
Saint John commands him to write, "Blessed are those who are
invited to the marriage supper of the Lamb," for these are the

---

[9] Ibid., 605.
[10] Ibid., 595, 599.

"true words of God" (Rev. 19:9). Thus, both the angel and the saints in heaven proclaim the commencement of the marriage supper of the Lamb.

The marriage supper, to which all the faithful are invited, represents the sacramental life of the Church Militant (cf. Rev. 20:4–6), centered on the Eucharist, which will last until the resurrection of the dead and the Last Judgment (cf. Rev. 20:11–15). After the Last Judgment, the Book of Revelation comes to its climax. The marriage of Christ and His bride, the Church, is consummated with "the holy city, new Jerusalem, coming down out of heaven from God, prepared as a bride adorned for her husband" (Rev. 21:2). The Church Suffering and the Church Triumphant have been resurrected (cf. Rev. 20:12–13) to join the Church Militant as a single bride upon the "new earth" (Rev. 21:1). The Messiah has finally wed "the Bride, the wife of the Lamb" (Rev. 21:9), the people of God fully purified and restored (cf. Rev. 21:22–27). The vision of the prophets is fulfilled, and the restoration of Israel is now complete (cf. Is. 65:17–18; 66:7–8).

Conclusion

The covenantal correspondence between human marriage and the union of God and His people is an essential element of divine revelation, set forth by the Old Testament prophets. The very deficiency of this union, so often betrayed by idolatry in Israel's history, points to the need for the Messiah, who alone could secure the union perfectly. Thus, the faithful cry out for the Messiah and long for His coming, as reflected in the allegorical sense of the Song of Songs. Jesus answers the cry of the faithful, revealing to His disciples that He is the divine Bridegroom drawing near to His wedding feast. The wedding feast begins with the Church's celebration of the Eucharist in the New Covenant and will last until the Last Judgment, after which the marriage of Christ and the Church is consummated. When the New Jerusalem comes down from heaven to the new earth, the restoration of the people of God will be complete.

Discussion Questions

1. Read Hos. 6:6. How do we practice the covenantal virtues of charity and knowledge in our own marriages?
2. What does God's covenant with His people teach us about the indissolubility of marriage?
3. Nearly half of all marriages today end in divorce, and many Americans do not bother to marry at all. What effect does the breakdown of marriage in our society have on Catholics' understanding of the Church?
4. How do contemporary societal notions of marriage undermine the truth of marriage as a covenant and sacrament?
5. How does the nuptial imagery of Scripture deepen our understanding of our personal vocations? How does this imagery enlighten our understanding of consecrated celibacy, as well as marriage?

Stephen Pimentel is the author of Witnesses of the Messiah: On the Acts of the Apostles 1-15 *(Emmaus Road Publishing, 2002) and* Envoy of the Messiah: On the Acts of the Apostles 16-28 *(Emmaus Road Publishing, 2005). He is also a contributor to* Catholic for a Reason III: Scripture and the Mystery of the Mass *(Emmaus Road Publishing, 2004) and has written for* Lay Witness *magazine. He holds a Master of Arts in theology from Christendom College.*

CHAPTER IX

Surprised by Love
Reflections on Pope Benedict XVI's First Encyclical

EDWARD AND ELIZABETH SRI

The topic of Pope Benedict XVI's first encyclical, *Deus Caritas Est*, caught many by surprise.[1] Moral relativism, secularization, abortion, liturgy—these are some of the themes people expected him to address.

But instead, this new pope—known for his intellect, scholarship, and courage to tackle controversial issues—chose to write on a topic quite simple, timeless, and appealing to all: the mystery of love.

What is immediately most striking about this move is its utter novelty. Never before had a papal encyclical been written specifically on the nature of love. Yet, in an age when so many people are struggling in their most fundamental relationships of love (in their marriages, families, dating relationships, etc.), the topic of Pope Benedict's encyclical is needed now more than ever. That is perhaps why at the beginning of his pontificate he wrote that he wanted to "clarify some essential facts" about the reality of human love.

---

[1] This chapter is adapted from an article that originally appeared in the Knights of Columbus magazine, *Columbia*. See E. Sri, "Surprised by Love" *Columbia* (May 2006).

The Two Loves

The Pope begins his teaching by noting how there is much confusion in the modern world over what the word "love" means. "Today, the term 'love' has become one of the most frequently used and misused of words, a word to which we attach quite different meanings" (no. 2). Indeed, in a culture like ours where a man can use the same word to describe his feelings about a favorite beer ("I love Guinness") or a favorite baseball team ("I love the Chicago Cubs") as he does to express his marital commitment to his wife ("I love you"), it's no wonder the word "love" is losing some of its profound meaning. What do we *really* mean when we speak of love?

To offer some clarification, the Pope first explains two key words that have been used throughout the centuries to describe love: *eros* and *agape*. *Eros* is commonly called "worldly love," and *agape* is love "grounded in and shaped by faith." *Eros* is "possessive love," a love that is self-seeking, pursuing its own pleasure or advantage in a relationship; while *agape* is a sacrificial love that selflessly seeks the good of the other person. *Eros* is that "love between man and woman which is neither planned nor willed but somehow imposes itself upon human beings" (no. 3). But *agape* is acquired through much effort, self-denial, and commitment to the other person.

For Pope Benedict, *eros* and *agape* represent two dimensions of the single reality of love. But there are many dangers when these two aspects are separated from each other.

For example, in pre-Christian cultures, *eros* was considered "a kind of intoxication" in which a man's emotions and passions became so powerful that they overwhelm his use of reason. And it was believed that supreme happiness was found by allowing one's self to be swept away by the romantic feelings and sensual desires of *eros*. Indeed, *eros* was considered a divine power: all other powers in heaven and earth pale in comparison to the power of *eros*. That is why yielding to these feelings was viewed as bringing man into a state of ecstasy—overcoming the isolation of one's self and experiencing fellowship with the divine.

While Pope Benedict emphasizes that *eros* itself is not bad, he does critique this pagan understanding of love as being "warped and destructive" (no. 4), for it focuses primarily on one's own feelings and desires and leaves out the sacrificial aspect of love that serves the other person's good (*agape*). "Love is not merely a sentiment," he writes. "Sentiments come and go. A sentiment can be a marvelous first spark, but it is not the fullness of love" (no. 17).

This has important implications for men and women today. For like the ancient Greeks, we, too, live in an era when love is primarily associated with feelings and sexual desire. Popular movies, television shows, and love songs constantly reinforce the association and get us to think that supreme happiness awaits us just around the corner if only we give in to our passions and emotions. In such an environment, it's no wonder that the Church's moral teachings on pre-marital sex and marriage are not understood by so many people in our world today. Why should I wait until marriage? Why should I suppress those feelings that will lead me to love and happiness? Why does the Church want to prevent me from experiencing love?

However, far from hindering love, the Church's teachings on sexuality actually help make true, lasting love possible. The Church challenges us to build our lives not on the fragile, unstable kind of love found primarily in sentiments that come and go (*eros*), but on the durable, committed, self-giving love (*agape*), which is the kind of love our hearts most deeply desire.

Along these lines, Pope Benedict wisely warns us that slavishly following the passions and emotions of *eros* is what prevents authentic love from developing. *Eros* may inspire hope for supreme happiness and desire for communion with another person, but it needs to be trained, directed, and purified. Left on its own, intoxicated and undisciplined *eros* collapses in on itself. *Eros* on its own is inward-looking, constantly seeking its own experience of romantic feelings and sensual pleasure. The man who remains at the level of undisciplined *eros* is not really able to love another person selflessly. He is so preoccupied over pursuing his own desires and pleasurable feelings in a relationship that he is not truly able to seek the woman's good for her own sake.

Love Needs to Be Healed

This is why the Pope emphasizes that "*eros* needs to be disciplined and purified if it is to provide not just fleeting pleasure, but a certain foretaste . . . of that beatitude for which our whole being yearns" (no. 4).

Here we come to the heart of Pope Benedict's teaching on human love. He tells us that *eros* must be healed if it is to mature and develop into the fullness of love. And the only way *eros* will be healed is through *agape*—self-giving love. He writes that love is indeed meant to be "ecstasy," but "not in the sense of a moment of intoxication," which is focused more on me—my own pleasure and good feelings. Rather, love is ecstasy in the sense of being a journey out of one's own selfishness. Benedict calls it "an ongoing exodus out of the closed inward-looking self towards its liberation through self-giving" (no. 6).

Indeed, the supreme happiness that *eros* drives me to seek is paradoxically found only when I move beyond selfish preoccupation with my own feelings and pleasure and live sacrificially for the other person's good. As Jesus says in the Gospels, "Whoever seeks to gain his life will lose it, but whoever loses his life will preserve it" (Lk. 17:33).

This is *agape* love. As Pope Benedict explains, "Love now becomes concern and care for the other. No longer is it self-seeking, a sinking in the intoxication of happiness; instead it seeks the good of the beloved. . . . It is ready, and even willing, for sacrifice" (no. 6).

Eros, with its self-centered tendencies, gradually becomes healed the more *agape* enters the picture. The more a person is willing to sacrifice his own comfort, preferences, and pleasure for the sake of serving his beloved's good, the stronger the relationship will be. Indeed, *eros* and *agape* are never meant to be completely separated. The passion of *eros* itself is meant to open up to the sacrificial, other-centered love of *agape*.

Even if *eros* is at first mainly covetous and ascending, a fascina-
tion for the great promise of happiness, in drawing near to the
other, it is less and less concerned with itself, increasingly seeks
the happiness of the other, is concerned more and more with the
beloved, bestows itself and wants to "be there for" the other. The
element of *agape* thus enters into this love, for otherwise *eros* is
impoverished and even loses its own nature. (no. 7)

But Pope Benedict emphasizes that man cannot live this sacrificial *agape* love all on his own power. "He cannot always give,
he must also receive," he writes (no. 7). Therefore, if we wish to
love others, we must constantly return to that ultimate source
for *agape* in our own lives: Jesus Christ. We will only be able to
truly love others here on earth to the extent that we are drinking
deeply from the love of God Himself.

Divine *Eros*

Now we arrive at what might be the most revolutionary
aspect of the encyclical: the way Pope Benedict explains God's
love as *eros*.

The Bible certainly reveals God as a divine power, the
source of all creation and the ordering principle of the universe.
However, the Bible also shows us that this Almighty Creator God
is at the same time a passionate lover, who loves us personally
"with all the passion of a true love" (no. 10).

Pope Benedict goes so far as to call God's love for humanity
"*eros*."

The Scriptures bear this out. While the Bible uses many images
to describe God's relationship with humanity (e.g., Lord, Creator,
Savior, Law-giver), the most intimate one is Bridegroom. In the Old
Testament, Yahweh comes to Israel not just as her Lord, but most
lovingly, as her Bridegroom. When Israel is faithful to the covenant,
she is described as God's spotless bride and faithful wife. When
Israel breaks God's commandments by worshipping other deities,
she is described as an unfaithful wife and adulteress. The Pope notes
how the Bible is comfortable using "boldly erotic images" (no. 9) to
describe God's passionate love for His people.

However, the Bible also demonstrates that this divine *eros* is completely perfected in *agape*. We can see this especially in the way God forgives Israel's sins. When Israel becomes an "adulteress" by breaking the covenant and worshipping other deities, human justice would conclude that she should be punished. In fact, the Law of Moses itself said that if Israel broke covenant with God, she would be handed over to the pagan nations and sent off into exile and slavery.

Yet, it is just at this point that God's love is revealed to be something much greater than human love. Consider the following passage from Hosea, which beautifully portrays God's passionate love for Israel as being so great that it overlooks the just punishments of the law:

> How can I give you up, O Ephraim!
>   How can I hand you over, O Israel! . . .
> My heart recoils within me,
>   my compassion grows warm and tender.
> I will not execute my fierce anger,
>   I will not again destroy Ephraim;
> for I am God and not man,
>   the Holy One in your midst. (Hos. 11:8–9)

Astonishingly, God's love for Israel is so powerful that it overcomes His justice. God so much desires to be in union with His people that He cannot deliver Israel over to her enemies forever. The pope explains: "God's passionate love for his people. . . . is at the same time a forgiving love. It is so great that it turns God against himself, his love against his justice" (no. 10). Here, God's *eros* is thus revealed as *agape*.

Pope Benedict also points out that this passage from Hosea pre-figures the mystery of the Cross, where God's *eros* and *agape* are revealed most fully. God so loved the human family that He passionately pursued us, became one of us, and even followed us into death, giving Himself completely on Calvary so that we might be reconciled with Him. On Good Friday, therefore, God's passionate love (*eros*) is shown in its greatest splendor as a completely sacrificial and self-giving love (*agape*). "The death on the cross is the culmination of that turning of God against himself in which he gives himself in order to raise man up and save him. This is love in its most radical form" (no. 12).

The Eucharist: Sacrament of Love

The fact that God's love is completely passionate and completely self-giving—total *eros* and total *agape*—has important implications for our lives because the divine perfection of *eros* in *agape* serves as the model for human love.

But how can we weak and sinful human beings imitate God's perfect love? Too often, our human love is trapped in *eros* and tainted by self-centeredness. A man may, for example, sincerely desire to love his wife with sacrificial, self-giving love. But in reality, he often falls very short of the mark, weighed down by his own selfishness, laziness, pride, and fear.

If left to our own powers, we would have no hope of fully reaching the level of *agape* in our marriages. But Pope Benedict reminds us that there is a higher love that can transform our hearts, our marriages, and all our relationships by making us love more like Christ. That divine love is found in the Eucharist.

When Catholics talk about the Eucharist, we commonly speak of the Real Presence of Jesus Christ and receiving His Body, Blood, Soul, and Divinity. But Pope Benedict goes a step further to note that when we receive Jesus in the Eucharist, we also "enter into the very dynamic of his self-giving" (no. 13). In other words, in Holy Communion, we become united to the same Body and Blood that Jesus offered up in perfect *agape* love for our sins. With Christ's very divine love in us through the Eucharist, our own self-centered, human love begins to be healed and to become ever more sacrificial like Christ's.

The Eucharist draws us into Jesus' act of self-oblation. More than just statically receiving the incarnate *Logos*, we enter into the very dynamic of his self-giving. The imagery of marriage between God and Israel is now realized in a way previously inconceivable:

it had meant standing in God's presence, but now it becomes union with God through sharing in Jesus' self-gift, sharing in his body and blood. (no. 13)

Pope Benedict goes on to note how in the early Church, the word *agape* actually became a term for describing the Eucharist. This is most fitting, for in the Eucharist, "God's own *agape* comes to us bodily, in order to continue his work in us and through us" (no. 14). And for most of us, there is an awful lot of work God needs to do in us so that we can love more and more like Him! Indeed, Holy Communion draws us out of ourselves and into His love, so that He may heal our weak, fallen human love—tainted as it is by selfishness and fear—and transform it with His perfect, divine, self-giving love.

Therefore, if we want stronger marriages and stronger relationships—if we want to move out of a predominantly self-seeking *eros* and toward an *eros* that is permeated by self-giving *agape*—we must turn to the source of perfect love in the Eucharist. For whenever we go to Mass, we enter into the mystery of Christ's passionate love for humanity (*eros*), which drove Him to total self-giving love for us on the cross (*agape*). It is in the Eucharist that our weak, fallen, selfish hearts are transformed the most by the totally passionate and totally self-giving love of Jesus Christ, giving us the power to love others far beyond what we could ever do on our own.

Discussion Questions

1. How do people tend to view love today?
2. How does Pope Benedict's description of authentic love differ from what the world says about love?
3. Explain in your own words the difference between *eros* and *agape*. What is the relationship between these two aspects of love?
4. What are some of the dangers of *eros*? How does *eros* on its own keep authentic, long-lasting love from developing?

5. Pope Benedict teaches that God's love is both *eros* and *agape*. How is this so? In what way do these two aspects of love come together in God's love for us? How is this a model for human love?

6. Take a moment to think about how you are falling short of agape love in your relationship with your spouse/fiancé. In what specific ways are you self-centered, seeking your own pleasure, comfort, and preferences rather than seeking to serve first the needs of your spouse/fiancé? What practical things can you do to grow in selfless, self-giving love?

Edward Sri, S.T.D., is professor of theology and scripture at the Augustine Institute's Masters in Catechesis and Evangelization program in Denver, Colorado. He is the author of several books including, Mystery of the Kingdom *(Emmaus Road) and a Catholic best-selling book on the Rosary,* The New Rosary in Scripture *(Servant).*

Elizabeth Sri served as one of the first missionaries in FOCUS (Fellowship of Catholic University Students) and has written and led several Bible studies. She is the mother of four children and a full-time homemaker.

CHAPTER X

Love Waiting to Give Itself
Biblical Insights on Marriage Preparation

MEI-LING AND RICHARD WHITE

Our next-door neighbor here in Atchison, Kansas is an assistant superintendent of schools. He has gone to college for eight years in preparation for this line of work. Our neighbor across the street is a lawyer and county attorney; he went to college for seven years, including three years of law school, to learn how to practice law. Another neighbor teaches physics and astronomy at Benedictine College. His post-high school education adds up to nine years! There is nothing out of the ordinary about this; in order to become a first-rate school superintendent, lawyer, or astronomer, proper training is essential. We all know that these occupations require years of preparation.

And yet, while the vocation of marriage is different from an occupation, nevertheless, we find nothing strange at all about couples getting married with absolutely no preparation at all! Or if there is any preparation, usually the focus is on planning for the wedding; a quick glance at bridal magazines in the checkout line at the grocery store confirms this. But are couples really ready for marriage merely by waltzing up to the altar and saying "I do," or does marriage too require training and preparation? Given the massive breakdown of the institution of marriage today, it is apparent that good marriage preparation is sorely needed. As John Paul II put it, "More than ever necessary in our times is preparation of young people for marriage and family life" (FC, no. 66).

This is urgent not only for couples entering marriage but also in order to deepen respect for marriage in our day. As the Pontifical Council for the Family says, "Marriage preparation must be set within the urgent need to evangelize culture—by permeating it to its *roots* . . . in everything that concerns the institution of marriage."[1] In order to carry out this task, it will be helpful to explore Scripture for wisdom concerning marriage preparation. In this chapter, we will look at some basic principles on this topic as found in God's Word.

To begin with, the process of marriage preparation is a process of discovering the fundamental nature, meaning, and dignity of marriage. When a couple exchanges vows on their wedding day, they must know what they are consenting to and thus need at least a basic understanding of the essential goods and properties of marriage. Marriage preparation is vital, then, for purposes of educating the spouses in regard to the *meaning* of marriage.

We are given a model of this process of self-discovery and awareness of the nature of marriage right at the beginning of Scripture in the person of Adam. The whole drama of Genesis 2 revolves around the finding of a suitable partner, a bride, for the first man, since it was "not good" that he be alone (Gen. 2:18). But instead of immediately presenting Adam with his bride as we might expect, God brings animals before the man so that he could name them. It is explained (as if we needed to be told) that no suitable partner from among the animals was found (Gen 2:20). While at first glance this passage may seem mysterious (did the Lord really expect Adam to find a bride among the hippos?), we like to look at the episode as the world's first pre-Cana class. In

---

[1] Pontifical Council for the Family, *Preparation for the Sacrament of Marriage* (May 13, 1996), 20.

naming the animals, the man learns an important lesson vital to his preparation for marriage—that he is utterly unique and that a suitable partner must share this uniqueness. Otherwise, he will be unable, humanly speaking, to make a gift of himself in love.

The man, then, is cast into a deep sleep and is awakened with his bride (literally) at his side. While many couples have followed Adam's example by going to sleep during pre-Cana sessions, few have woken up, like Adam, actually ready for marriage! His enthusiastic cry of approval ("This at last is bone of my bones and flesh of my flesh [Gen. 2:23]) when confronted with his bride expresses an important moment of self-discovery. The man learns the purpose of his vocation: to make a gift of himself in love. Indeed, as the man and woman realize by gazing upon one another, they were created "for the other." "Therefore a man leaves his father and his mother and cleaves to his wife, and they become one flesh" (Gen. 2:24).

Before the formation of the woman, on the other hand, the man had no one to give himself to, and this was "not good" indeed. Thus, the man and woman—equal in dignity and nature—are called to give themselves to one another, a fact expressed through their complementarity. This is the fundamental *truth* of marriage that every couple must learn and live out: each is called to make a gift of self to the other. In a sense, the process of marriage preparation is tied to this truth because it will be successful to the extent that each partner is generous to the other even before marriage. The period of marriage preparation is really an "apprenticeship" for the couple in "love as self-giving."

If preparation for marriage means formation in "love as self-giving," then how, practically speaking, do couples accomplish this? First, by acquiring and nurturing the virtue of chastity. Our society tends to think of chastity in negative terms as merely the decision to refrain from sexual activity. While chastity does require this choice before marriage, it has to do more with coming into possession of ourselves and integrating our sexual desires and passions into a gift of authentic love. If we do not have mastery over our sexual desires, how then can we make a free gift of our sexuality? For we cannot give that which we do not possess. As the Pontifical Council for the Family states, "Chastity is not a mortification of love but rather a condition for real love. In fact, if the vocation to married love is a vocation to self-giving in marriage, one must succeed in possessing oneself in order to be able to truly give oneself."[2]

The period of marriage preparation, therefore, is an opportunity for couples to nurture chastity and thus prepare to become great lovers. For when they become married, the call to chastity remains. What changes is the manner in which chastity is lived out. Having channeled their sexual desires and passions into an authentic gift of love for the other during the marriage preparation period, the couple is truly ready to "make love" on their wedding night.

Turning to Scripture, we find examples of both chastity and unchastity during the marriage preparation stage, and their respective consequences. Genesis 34 contains an episode about Shechem, a Hivite prince. He apparently had genuine affection for Dinah, daughter of Leah and Jacob, and wanted to marry her out of love: "And his soul was drawn to Dinah the daughter of Jacob; he loved the maiden and spoke tenderly to her" (Gen. 34:3). And yet, his decision to have unlawful relations with her (in this case, rape) was not worthy of this love. The fiasco that followed, including Shechem's murder at the hands of Dinah's brothers, is perhaps indicative of the destructive consequences of unchastity. In our society, unchastity during the marriage preparation period often takes the form of pre-marital sex and cohabitation. To be sure, most couples who refuse to cease "living together" before marriage have the best intentions and really do love one another. However, their love, in this case, is misguided, for the decision to cohabitate is actually destructive of love. Indeed, while chastity is training in selflessness, unchastity is training in selfishness. Given the opportunity to nurture chastity for the sake of authentic love before marriage, cohabitating couples are actually motivated out

---

[2] *Preparation for the Sacrament*, 24.

of lust. Indeed, they plant the seeds of destruction of marriage by not giving chastity a chance to take root. Pre-marital sex short-circuits the process whereby the couple learns to gain mastery of their sexual desires and thus become free. As the author of the Song of Solomon so beautifully states, "I adjure you, O daughters of Jerusalem, by the gazelles or the hinds of the field, that you stir not up nor awaken love until it please" (Song 3:5).

On the other hand, the Bible shows the positive consequences of pre-marital chastity. Tobiah was deeply in love with Sarah before their marriage (Tob. 6:17) but never let his desire for her turn to lust. In fact, his prayer on their wedding night is one of the most beautiful in the Bible and points to the nobility and splendor of chastity:

> Blessed are thou, O God of our fathers, and blessed be thy holy and glorious name forever. Let the heavens and all thy creatures bless thee. Thou madest Adam and gavest him Eve his wife as a helper and support. From them the race of mankind has sprung. Thou didst say, "It is not good that the man should be alone; let us make a helper for him like himself." And now, O Lord, I am not taking this sister of mine because of lust, but with sincerity. Grant that I may find mercy and may grow old together with her. And she said with him, "Amen." Then they both went to sleep for the night. (Tob. 8:5–9)

Couples entering marriage should make this prayer their own. Indeed, growing in chastity is one of the greatest gifts that can be made to one's beloved during the marriage preparation period and leads to a solid foundation for marriage.

Another vital component of formation during the marriage preparation period is the diligent practice of prayer. Sarah's prayers were heard in heaven and gave rise to the chain of events leading to her marriage to Tobiah (Tob. 3:16–17). Mary's prayerful reception of God's word during her betrothal to Joseph (Lk. 1:38) led to the very Incarnation of Christ and the salvation of mankind! The Lord hears the prayers of couples preparing for marriage and will mightily bless those who avail themselves to His presence. "The dignity and responsibility of the Christian family as the domestic

Church," John Paul II says, "can be achieved only with God's unceasing aid, which will surely be granted if it is humbly and trustingly petitioned in prayer"(FC, no. 59).

Given that marriage preparation is a "formation in self-giving," it is not surprising that the Bible shows one or both of the partners making significant acts of self-denial for the good of their beloved and future marriage. For example, Rebekah chose to leave her father and mother and travel a great distance with Abraham's servant for the sake of her future husband Isaac (Gen. 24:58), even though it would have been more convenient for her to have simply stayed at home. Isaac and Rebekah's son Jacob pushed the bar even further. He worked seven years for his future father-in-law Laban in order to marry Rachel (and to think that couples complain that pre-Cana sessions are too long). As if that were not enough, he labored an additional seven years to gain Rachel's hand after accidentally marrying Rachel's sister Leah! Jacob is an example to all couples that marriage prepara- tion requires effort and sacrifice (and hopefully sobriety on one's wedding night).

Other examples abound. In the Book of Ruth, Naomi and her daughter-in-law Ruth were left destitute after their husbands died (Ruth 1:21) and were even forced to put their land up for sale (Ruth 4:3). According to Jewish law, the next of kin had a right and duty to restore the land of an impoverished relative by buying it back (Lev. 25:25) and to marry a deceased relative's widow who had died without leaving male offspring (Deut. 25:5–6). The so- called "kinsman redeemer" in this case was Boaz, who carried out this duty at considerable sacrifice. Not only did Boaz agree, out of loving kindness, to marry the foreigner Ruth, he also purchased Naomi's land at significant cost to himself. For her part, Ruth gave up everything to follow Naomi from Moab to Naomi's hometown of Bethlehem and to take Boaz for her husband. Happily, both partners willingly made these sacrifices, and God blessed them with a son Obed, from whom David descended. As for David, he risked life and limb to marry Michal by going into battle against an army of Philistines (1 Sam. 18:25–27). And consider the risk taken by Tobiah to marry Sarah. Her previous six husbands all died on the wedding night—little wonder he offered a prayer before retiring with Sarah for the evening! Joseph took Mary as his wife despite her becoming pregnant during the betrothal period. In doing so, he risked considerable humiliation in the eyes of society.

While some of these examples might seem far removed from our experience, they, nonetheless, remind us that individuals are called to acts of love and self-sacrifice for the good of their marriage not only during marriage but also in preparation for marriage. Indeed, as John Paul II says, "This reciprocal giving of self reveals the spousal nature of love."[3] For if marriage requires mutual giving, what better way for couples to prepare for the Sacrament than to practice generosity before saying "I do." What this actually involves might be different for every couple, and we have already emphasized the importance of nurturing chastity and prayer. But this could also mean simply keeping an open heart and mind during pre-Cana classes, showing patience in planning for the wedding, or keeping the lines of communication open.

The Bible contains a negative example of this in the person of Samson. Against the advice of his parents, Samson chose to marry a Philistine woman (Judg. 14:3), and a seven-day wedding feast was given in honor of the event. During the celebration, however, Samson made himself the focus of the occasion by posing an obscure riddle to his companions and apparently ignoring the needs of his bride (Judg. 14:12); for her part, she left Samson and married his best man at the wedding (Judg. 14:20)! While there are many lessons here (e.g. that the best man can become the worst man), the episode reminds us that we should seek the good of our beloved in all things and not focus on our own wants and needs; this is especially important for couples entering marriage.

In the end, couples who use the period of marriage preparation as a time of formation in "love as self-giving" are really following the supreme example of Jesus Christ. In a sense, His

---

[3] John Paul II, *Letter to Families* (February 2, 1994, Libreria Editrice Vaticana), 11.

entire public ministry—beginning with His presence at a wedding in Cana of Galilee— was a preparation for His espousal of the Church. He loved His future bride, the Church, so much that He laid down His life for her (Eph. 5:25), and she was formed out of His pierced side. Jesus invites every couple to follow in His footsteps and to drink abundantly of that best wine, His Eucharistic Body and Blood, that He the Bridegroom has saved for last.

As couples become more closely united with Jesus, they become more and more prepared for marriage. As the Pontifical Council for the Family states, "Since Christian love is purified, perfected and elevated by Christ's love for the Church (cf. GS, 49), the engaged should imitate this model and develop their awareness of self-giving which is always connected with the mutual respect and self-denial that help this love grow."[4] Ultimately, every sacramental marriage is rooted in Jesus' love for the Church. The more couples become united with the Bridegroom before marriage, therefore, the more their own marriage will be a sign to the world of God's loving presence to humanity. To again quote the Pontifical Council for the Family, "It would be desirable if the favorable moment of marriage preparation could be transformed, as a sign of hope, into a new evangelization."[5]

In a sense, it would be true to say that the process of marriage preparation actually continues after marriage. For if marriage preparation is training in "love as self-giving," the real workout begins with marriage! Of course, one day the sacrament will give way to the reality and there will be no more giving and taking in marriage (Mt. 22:30). But until then, we are like the ten virgins preparing for a great wedding feast indeed (Mt. 25:1). Couples who are well prepared for marriage, like the five wise virgins, possess an abundant source of oil for their lamps. May the truth, goodness, and beauty of Christian marriage be respected and shine for all to see.

---

[4] *Preparation for the Sacrament*, 40.
[5] Ibid, 2.

Discussion Questions

1. Marriage preparation means different things to different people. How does our society view marriage preparation? What does marriage preparation mean to you?
2. Why do we need marriage preparation?
3. What is the virtue of chastity? Why is the practice of chastity vital during the marriage preparation period?
4. What are some other things couples can do to better prepare for marriage?

Mei-Ling and Richard White reside in Atchison, Kansas with their three children. Mei-Ling is a full-time homemaker and Richard is an Associate Professor and Chair of the Department of Theology at Benedictine College. He holds a PhD from Marquette University and is contributing author of Catholic for a Reason I. *The Whites teach marriage preparation classes for their parish.*

CHAPTER XI

Super-Natural
Family Planning

CURTIS AND MICHAELANN MARTIN

It is a wonderful thing when your fourteen-year-old son can teach you something about chastity. It happened just the other day. We were talking about an upcoming conference on sexual purity for young people. Michaelann asked him if he was interested in attending this year's conference (he and his brother both went last year). I told him that we weren't going to make him go but we would make every effort to send him if he were interested. He responded, "I'm open to going, but last year it was only about abstinence." Not sure of his point, I quickly countered, "That's right, chastity for single people is abstinence." He paused for a moment and then responded, "Abstinence is what you do or don't do with your body, but Jesus called us to more; He called us to be pure from the heart." As we listened to the wisdom of our son, we saw the wonderfully distinctive character of Christ's call to the moral life. Our actions, if they are to be truly pleasing to our Heavenly Father, must not be mere external obedience to a law; our obedience should manifest faithfulness from the heart.

This discussion with our son is a wonderful example of what we hope to accomplish with this chapter. We want to begin by praising the right teaching and practice of Natural Family Planning, but we want to go beyond the practice of NFP to the heart of the matter.

Marriage is a unique Sacrament, because it has a natural existence that pre-dates Christ. Indeed, it pre-dates the Old Testament and finds its origin in the creation of the first man and woman. Jesus takes the natural reality of marriage and He heals, restores, and elevates it to a Sacrament of the New Covenant. In Christ, marriage, which has a supernatural origin, takes on a super-natural aspect. It is because of the sacramental nature of Christian marriage that we hope to deepen the discussion of responsible parenting with a reflection on "Super-Natural Family Planning."

What Am I Doing on Earth for Heaven's Sake?

This is a question every married person should ask themselves. The day-to-day realities of paying bills, raising children, making a living, and trying to survive can overtake the more fundamental questions. What does our marriage mean in light of heaven? Do we see our marriage and family as our primary pathway to Jesus Christ? Do we see the dignity and nobility of the calling entrusted to us by Almighty God as parents?

The Catechism of the Catholic Church introduces the sacraments by speaking of their mystery.

> Such is the mystery of Christ revealed and fulfilled in history according to the wisely ordained plan that Saint Paul calls the "plan of the mystery"[1] and the patristic tradition will call the "economy of the Word incarnate" or the "economy of salvation." (CCC 1066)

The word "economy" has nothing to do with finances, at least directly. Economy is the *oikos-nomos* (Greek), literally, the household policy or laws that affect every Christian who has been brought into covenant with the living God. God's plan for us is a mystery, according to the Scriptures. A mystery, not in the sense that our life's purpose is unknowable, but in the sense that we

---

[1] Eph. 1:9.

have been called to something so rich, so beautiful that we will never be able to fully comprehend the dignity and splendor to which we have been invited.

Like swimming in the ocean, each of us can master the skills necessary to thrive in marriage, yet none of us can plumb the depths over which we pass. Marriage is a sacrament of the New Covenant—a mystery that, in fact, gives us the grace to accomplish our sublime calling. It is only with a supernatural perspective that we can realize the noble dignity to which we have been called, and only within the mystery that we can come to appreciate our mission on this earth for Heaven's sake.

A supernatural perspective is also needed for couples who are unable to conceive children. God has a plan for each of us in marriage. He asks for our hearts to be open to life and His holy will, which may mean accepting childlessness as our God-given path. A couple unable to have children are called to foster heroic generosity in a unique way. Only by trusting God and submitting our will to His can we know the specific calling that He has uniquely prepared for each of us.

A Renewal of Culture

There is a great debate in our modern culture—a culture divided between the proponents of life and the harbingers of death. We live in a society almost evenly divided between those who, under the banner of "pro-choice" call for the "right" to kill children while they are still resting in the womb of their mother, and those who see life as a gift given by the Lord of life and therefore sacred and worthy of our awe. We are told in Psalm 127:3–5:

> Children too are a gift from the LORD, the fruit of the womb, a reward. Like arrows in the hand of a warrior are the children born in one's youth. Blessed are they whose quivers are full. They will never be shamed contending with foes at the gate. (NAB)

Marriage is the sacred mystery within which human life is ordained to be conceived, nurtured, cultivated, and lived.

Those of us who speak in favor of life must speak with a united voice if we would desire to be heard. Our Lord Himself prophesied that it would be the unity and love that His followers had for one another that would be the clear sign that we are His disciples (cf. John 13:35). And yet, there has been great division even within the Church concerning this most noble aspect of marital love.

In the late 1960s Pope Paul VI restated the ancient and unchanging teaching of Christ and His Church that all forms of contraception were contrary to the will of God and human nature. For nearly two millenniums all monotheists (Christians, Jews, and Moslems), had rejected contraception as being gravely immoral.

However, in 1930 the Anglican community broke with the historical teaching and said that in rare and serious occasions contraception might be tolerated. Pandora's Box was opened, and the line of attack for the sexual revolution had been laid. Within a generation, contraception and abortion were commonplace and a collective historical amnesia drew otherwise faithful Christians into open rebellion against the unwavering truth about the meaning of marital love.

The Devil is a shrewd and terrible foe. His military tactics resemble those of the most cunning tyrants; *divide and conquer* is a time-tested strategy. The rebellion of the sexual revolution caused a significant portion of Christians to fall into error on the sacredness of the life-giving aspects of the marital act. Scandalously, they were lead into error by some of their "shepherds;" in many cases, priests and theologians lead the way in the dissent. With what can, at best, be perceived as a "false compassion," an apparent majority of western couples refused their God-given call to be open to life.

Christians are meant to be the salt of the earth, and when that salt loses its savor it is of no use. Nothing remains to keep the culture on the right path. Within a generation, one in three children was killed in their mother's womb through surgical abortion, contraception became the norm, and untold millions of children were exterminated by the aborting effects of most contraceptive methods. Divorce, cohabitation, homosexuality, pornography, and abuse have all become pandemic thanks to this demonic trend. The Church warned that a rejection of God's will would unravel our culture. To witness how far we have fallen in such a short time is overwhelming.

In response to this hellish devastation, the Church has reiterated the Gospel of life. Faithful Catholics have worked tirelessly and heroically to articulate the Church's teachings. Groups like the Couple to Couple League have offered wonderful teachings about the nature of marriage and the importance of remaining true to the moral principles concerning marriage and family. The truth about Natural Family Planning (NFP) is being proclaimed, and many couples have discovered that living in accord with the Natural Law and remaining true to the Church's teachings is not only possible, but may also be the occasion for a renewal and deepening of spousal love.

So What's the Difference Anyway?

So why all the fuss? Aren't we splitting hairs here? After all, isn't NFP just the Church-approved form of contraception? Not at all! NFP is a method of recognizing a woman's natural cycle of fertility and intentionally acting in light of these cycles to either achieve or postpone pregnancy. At first glance, there are some cosmetic similarities but, in fact, there are substantial differences.

The marital act is, by its very nature, ordered to the procreation of children. Contraception is a separate act that seeks to render the marital act sterile; this second act is the problem. With NFP, there is only the decision to engage in the marital act or not. A couple is not required to have relations at any given moment, only to realize that when they do, they are participating in an act that God has designed and that He may bless with the gift of new life.[2]

---

[2] For faithful information about NFP we recommend contacting The Couple to Couple League, PO Box 111184, Cincinnati, OH 45211, (513) 471-2000, www.ccli.org.

Pope Paul VI affirmed the distinction between contraception and NFP in his encyclical *Humanae Vitae*:

> If then, there are serious motives to space out births, which derive from the physical or psychological conditions, the Church teaches that it is then licit to take into account the natural rhythms immanent in the generative functions, for the use of marriage in the infecund periods only, and in this way to regulate birth without offending the moral principles which have been recalled earlier. (HV, no. 16)

Archbishop Charles Chaput, OFM Cap., highlights the fundamental difference between contraception and NFP.

> Contraception is a choice, by any means, to sterilize a given act of intercourse. . . . Natural Family Planning is in no way contraceptive. The choice to abstain from a fertile act of intercourse is completely different from willful choice to sterilize a fertile act of intercourse.[3]

When NFP is practiced correctly, there is an awareness of God's plan and the possibility of bringing another soul into this world through our marital love, even when, for serious reasons, we may be attempting to avoid conception. Part of our discernment as a Christian couple is to recognize that God has called us to marriage for a purpose. Our love is God-given and is a good in and of itself; we are sanctified as we love each other. However, marital love, by its very nature, is ordered towards procreation (this is why homosexual unions can never be marriages and why contraception is such an offense to marriage). The honor of being married brings with it the office and duty (Latin; *munus*[4]). We have been called to love one another in our marriage by our heavenly Father, and His first command has never been revoked: "Be fruitful and multiply" (Gen. 1:28).

The Catechism puts it this way:

---

[3] Archbishop Charles Chaput, "On Human Life: A Pastoral Letter" (Denver: Office of Marriage and Family Life, Archdiocese of Denver, 1998), 13.

[4] For a clear discussion of the term "munus" see Janet Smith, *Humanae Vitae: A Generation Later* (Washington D.C.: CUA Press, 1991), 136–148.

A particular aspect of this responsibility concerns the *regulation of births*. For just reasons, spouses may wish to space the births of their children. It is their duty to make certain that their desire is not motivated by selfishness but is in conformity with the generosity appropriate to responsible parenthood. Moreover, they should conform their behavior to the objective criteria of morality:

> When it is a question of harmonizing married love with the responsible transmission of life, the morality of the behavior does not depend upon sincere intention and evaluation of motives alone; but it must be determined by objective criteria, criteria drawn from the nature of the person and his acts, criteria that respect the total meaning of mutual self-giving and human procreation in the context of true love; this is possible only if the virtue of married chastity is practiced with sincerity of heart. (CCC 2368, emphasis in the original)

We are instructed to conform our behavior to the objective criteria of morality. Pope Paul VI has helped us to see in which areas of our lives we might experience serious difficulties.

> In relation to physical, economic, psychological and social conditions, responsible parenthood is exercised, either by the deliberate and generous decision to raise a numerous family, or by the decision made for grave motives and with respect for the moral law, to avoid for the time being, or even for an indeterminate period, a new birth. . . . The responsible exercise of parenthood implies, therefore, that husband and wife recognize fully their duties towards God, towards themselves, towards the family and towards society, in a correct hierarchy of values. (HV, no. 10)

Nowhere does the pope mention the need for a vacation home or a new jet ski as sufficient reasons to avoid a pregnancy.

Apparent Similarities but Substantial Differences

So what is Super-Natural Family Planning (SNFP)? A couple practicing SNFP is aware of what is involved in NFP, but they also have their eyes on a supernatural end. A couple utilizing SNFP is actively engaging their intellects and wills and their minds and hearts, which have been elevated by supernatural insight and grace. They do not ignore the sufferings and serious difficulties that sometimes arise within married life, and they responsibly consider the use of NFP. However, their supernatural perspective and heroic generosity call them to live in the present moment. They do not let anxieties and reservations about an uncertain future shake their trust in their Heavenly Father. After all, we are a people who daily pray, "Give us *this* day our daily bread." SNFP says, "If God is providing for our daily needs now, and there are no certain limitations coming in the future, then we ought to trust that He will continue to care for our needs tomorrow."

The need for active trust in God is a foundational point in SNFP. As a sacrament, our marriage should reflect the victory of Christ over original sin. Listen to the Catechism describe the incompatibility between trust and sin:

> Man, tempted by the devil, let his trust in his Creator die in his heart and, abusing his freedom, disobeyed God's command. This is what man's first sin consisted of. All subsequent sin would be disobedience toward God and a lack of trust in His goodness. (CCC 397)

We have seen that there is a superficial similarity and a substantial difference between NFP and contraception; so too, there is a superficial similarity and substantial difference between SNFP and what might be labeled the error "Providentialism." Those who favor the use of NFP as a norm, even when serious reasons for avoiding a pregnancy do not exist, tend to criticize SNFP as falling into the error of "Providentialism." The "Providentialist" relies on God's care, however, without making recourse to the natural tools we have been given by God; he would think that a pregnancy will only take place if God has already planned on personally providing for all of the child's needs. The "Providentialist" would ignore existing serious problems with his health, finances, emotional or social concerns, and discern God's will in an overly simplistic manner; if a pregnancy happened, it must be God's will. This is a half truth; of course all life is God's will, but He also wills that we act as responsible collaborators in welcoming new life. This is where SNFP and Providentialism differ.

To fall into Providentialism is a bit like the man who lived in a flood zone. As the waters rose some men in a truck came by and offered him a ride out of the danger zone. He replied, "No thank you, I trust God will save me." A bit later, as the waters were rising, some rescuers came by in a boat and again offered to take him to safety. Again, he refused, "No thank you, God will save me." When the waters had flooded his home and he was trapped on the roof of his house, a helicopter lowered a ladder in a desperate effort to save him. Defiantly, he repeated, "No! I have faith! God will save me." Not too much later he was standing before Almighty God. He complained, "Lord, I trusted you to save me. Why did you abandon me?" God responded, "I sent you a truck, a boat, and a helicopter! What did you expect?" God wants us to communicate with Him and do our part.

It is true, as the Catechism affirms, "God is the sovereign master of his plan." However, the Catechism continues, "But to carry it out he also makes use of his creatures' cooperation. This use is not a sign of weakness, but rather a token of almighty God's greatness and goodness." (CCC 306). The error of the Providentialist is that he refuses to use his God-given intellect and will to exercise responsible parenthood.

Responsible parenting requires that we examine our circumstances honestly, but with an eye on the supernatural. A young couple will think after the birth of their first child, "We don't know if we could love a second child as much." In some ways they are right, because they have not yet been given the grace to love a second child; that grace comes with the conception, pregnancy, and birth of the next child. In other words the grace will come when we need it, not before we need it. That being said, we must also understand that God's children walk the path of the Cross, and, at times in our lives, our current sufferings and hardships may present serious difficulties; to bring children into those difficulties without thoughtful and prayerful reflection might be irresponsible. If Dad's business is closing in four months and he will lose his job, or if Mom is suffering from a serious ailment, this may very well lead a responsible couple to utilize natural methods to postpone a pregnancy. Once the storm passes, they can put aside the charting and rhythmic abstinence.

Grace Elevates Nature

The Church teaches that supernatural grace presupposes and elevates nature. Natural Family Planning recognizes the nature of married couples, and Super-Natural Family Planning focuses upon the supernatural character of human persons redeemed in Christ. Spouses and children are seen in light of their supernatural end, which is to live forever in heaven with God. Spouses are not just partners in the day-to-day activities of life; they are collaborators in one another's sanctification.

Natural wisdom, for example, tells us to take care of our bodies by eating right and exercising. Supernatural wisdom tells us that our body is meant to serve our soul, so we might fast and mortify our flesh for a greater spiritual good. So, too, "Natural" Family Planning may lead us to pursue certain natural goods such as wealth and physical comfort. "Super-Natural" Family Planning will lead us to pursue the greater goods of our supernatural calling and place natural goods at the service of supernatural goods for the sake of holiness. With a supernatural perspective we may be moved to welcome another child into our family because we have come to see that our children are destined to spend eternity with the Blessed Trinity.

For example, Curtis and I both grew up in southern California near the beach. We now live hundreds of miles away from the beach in Colorado. When we take vacations, we always seem to end up on the shore. We have found it to be restful and relaxing. We love walking along the sandy coastline as the waves splash our feet and playing in the surf with our children. Enjoying the beautiful sunsets and renewing our spirits are natural realities of our times on the coast. We truly have great family time while on these vacations. Naturally speaking, we would love to have a vacation home on the beach and if we had only two children, we would probably be able to own one. However, these goods do not compare with the dignity and awesome calling we have been given: to welcome, love, and form the children whom God has given us. In our lives, the natural good of having a beach house has been subordinated to the supernatural good of welcoming, loving, and raising our children.

Divine revelation has helped us to see that our marital love is created by God to welcome new life into the world, and that our children, in turn, draw us closer to one another and God. The Church declared unequivocally at Vatican II:

> Marriage and conjugal love are by their nature ordained toward begetting and educating children. Children are really the supreme gift of marriage and contribute very substantially to the welfare of their parents. (GS, no. 50)

A supernatural vision helps us to see that God is asking us to be open to new life because He wants our children to be instruments in our own sanctification.

Responsible Parenting

A point of disagreement may arise as to whether NFP ought to be practiced as an ordinary matter of course. Should married couples who are not experiencing serious difficulties be practicing NFP? We would ask "why?" We live in a very empirical culture, and science has provided many blessings to the modern world, but some things don't belong under the microscope; love is one of these things. Marriage is a mystery of love and of life. Michaelann is at one and the same time wife *and* mother; and Curtis is husband *and* father. When there are no serious reasons, there is no cause to separate what God has joined. The Sacrament of Marriage is designed in such a way as to express our love as an awe-inspiring unity, unless some serious challenge causes us to take a more analytical approach.

A physician is quoted in Kimberly Hahn's *Life-Giving Love*:

> I do not believe NFP is necessary or desirable for most married people. I do believe everyone should know about it, and about

where to learn the method if necessary, but I really don't think everyone needs to know all the details about how to do it, much less practice it. I disagree with those who say every woman should chart her cycles. Such a preoccupation with physiology is abnormal.

An analogy might be a food diary, where someone writes down every morsel consumed. This might be necessary for someone with diabetes, allergies, or severe obesity, but would be considered obsessive-compulsive for someone without a nutritional problem. In sexuality, where the interpersonal relationship is so important, such preoccupation with the physical may even be more harmful. Since NFP, i.e., periodic abstinence for the purpose of avoiding pregnancy, is appropriate only "for grave reasons," that is in the cases of dire necessity, it is an unhealthy focus on bodily functions for those who have no such grave necessity."[5]

Some would say that it is helpful to practice NFP when you first get married. This is an odd conclusion given the nature of Christian marriage. It would make more sense to say, "if you have serious reasons for avoiding a pregnancy, you *might* have serious reasons for postponing your wedding." There will be exceptions, but ordinarily responsible people get married when they are ready to begin a family. The defining aspect of the vocation to marriage is the marital act which is deigned by God to lead to new life. What would we think of a priest who opted not to offer Mass for the first few years of his priesthood so that he would have time to get to know his parishioners better? It is precisely in living our vocation that we are perfected in Christ.

The blessing of children is a God-given gift to spouses. Our children create a spouse-shaped hole in our heart. When we live heroic generosity in marriage, we give ourselves to one another and to our children and our longing for our spouse is perfected. When you see your spouse love and care for your children, the natural attraction and desire to be with him/her increases. Friends of ours recently told us of a family reunion; the kids were now grown and had come there with their spouses and children. Most of the couples had been drawn into the culture: DITTOs, "double

---

[5] Kimberly Hahn, *Life Giving Love: Embracing God's Beautiful Design for Marriage* (Cincinnati, OH: Servant Publications, 2001), 171.

income two to three offspring." They were tan, in great shape, and looking good. One couple was living the Church's vision for family life, and had their five children with them. They were a bit tired, a bit out of shape, and not as well-off financially, but throughout the reunion they were the one couple who habitually exchanged signs of affection. It may seem counter-intuitive, but it is not what you look like, it is how you give yourself in love that renders you attractive. We have always thought this from our own experience, but now there are studies that state these same results: "Studies show that when couples stretch their comfort zones for the sake of their children, romantic love increases in their relationship."[6] God designed marriage and, when it is lived rightly, it works.

This love for our spouse is a reflection of the love and appreciation we have for God. "Conjugal love reveals its true nature and nobility when it is considered in its supreme origin, God, who is love" (HV, no. 8). Or, as Pope John Paul II, recalling the words of the Second Vatican Council, frequently reminded us, "man can fully discover his true self only in a sincere giving of himself" (GS, no. 24). When we are humbled before God and dependent upon His gifts, we tend to stay closer to Him and have greater peace while living day to day.

We have made it a habit of trying to seek out couples and families that radiate joy in their marriage and family life. After spending time with them, we have noticed that they have two things in common: a steadfast love for God and His Church, and a desire to live their faith with integrity in the various aspects of their lives. Growing in our supernatural outlook has been a great joy for us and our family. As our children mature, we see how our struggle to remain faithful in a faithless world is benefiting them and their decisions. God doesn't want our blind obedience, He wants our heart! The best way to show God our love is in our actions. God has not necessarily called us to extraordinary things. But the ordinary sacrifices for the sake of love, within our sacramental marriage, become extraordinary gifts to God.

---

6 Gregory K. Popcak, MSW, LSW, *Faith and Family*, Winter 2002, p. 55.

Discussion Questions

1. What does your marriage mean in light of your heavenly destiny?

2. Do you see your marriage as a means for sanctifying yourself, your spouse, and your children by being true to your marriage vows? How do you live this reality out in daily life?

3. Are there areas of your married life that you need to entrust to God?

4. When in your married life have you experienced serious challenges in these four areas: Physical, economic, psychological, and social conditions?

5. How does a supernatural perspective affect your view of serious difficulties?

6. Do you know a couple/family that radiate their faith in their home in a joyful way? How might you deepen your relationship with them so that they could mentor you?

Curtis Martin is President and Founder of FOCUS, the Fellowship of Catholic University Students. He is co-author of Boys to Men: The Transforming Power of Virtue *and a contributing author for the* Catholic for a Reason *series.*

Michaelann Martin is author of Woman of Grace: A Bible Study for Married Women.

Together Curtis and Michaelann have co-authored Family Matters: A Biblical Study on Marriage and Family. *In 2004 they were honored by Pope John Paul II with the Benemerenti Award for their service to the Church. They have seven children.*

CHAPTER XII

Milk and Mystery
On Breastfeeding and the Theology of the Body

TERRI AND MIKE AQUILINA

A woman's voice broke the hush that had fallen over the crowd: "Blessed is the womb that bore you, and the breasts that you sucked" (Lk. 11:27).

This spontaneous cry, recorded in Saint Luke's Gospel, echoes even today. According to Pope John Paul II, it is a lasting praise "of motherhood, of femininity, of the female body in its typical expression of creative love."[1]

"Blessed the breasts that nursed you." Why would this woman, so dazzled by truth, cry out in tribute—not to the Preacher or His preaching—but to His mother and her mothering? The woman in the crowd knew intuitively that the love she encountered in the Messiah could be traced back to a great and generous mother's love. She spoke from her heart a truth that many mothers know: a breastfeeding woman is blessed, and so is her child.

---

[1] Pope John Paul II, General Audience, March 12, 1980.

Breastfeeding in the Bible

In the biblical world, a blessing arrives as God's reward for human fidelity to the requirements of the covenant. The Bible mentions breastfeeding often, and always as a blessing. On realizing that she would bear Isaac, the elderly matriarch Sarah spoke in the same terms as the anonymous woman of Luke's gospel: "God has made laughter for me; Who would have said to Abraham that Sarah would suckle children? Yet I have borne him a son in his old age" (Gen. 21:6–7). At the end of the Book of Genesis, the patriarch Jacob proclaimed nursing motherhood among the greatest blessings of the covenant:

> God Almighty . . . will bless you
> with blessings of heaven above,
> . . . blessings of the breasts and of the womb. (Gen. 49:25)

The counterpart to a blessing, however, is a curse. A breach of the covenant could bring down God's wrath in the form of afflictions—covenant curses—and these usually appear as an inversion of the covenant blessings. A plentiful harvest is a blessing, for example, while a famine is a curse. So, just as birth and breastfeeding are prominent among the covenant blessings, chief among the curses are, according to the Prophet Hosea, "a miscarrying womb and dry breasts" (Hos. 9:14), representing sterility, barrenness, and the end of the family line.

The norm throughout the ancient Near East was to breastfeed a child from birth until the third (or fourth) birthday.[2] The mother of the seven martyrs in the Second Book of Maccabees exhorts her youngest son to courage: "My son, have pity on me. I carried you nine months in my womb, and nursed you for three years" (2 Mac. 7:27). The legal requirements for priestly service seem to

---

[2] See, for example, Patricia Stuart-Macadam and Katherine A. Dettwyler, *Breastfeeding: Biocultural Perspectives* (Hawthorne, New York: Aldine de Gruyter, 1995), p. 64. See also Helen Wessel, *Natural Childbirth and the Christian Family* (New York: Harper & Row, 1983), 271–272. For more biblical and patristic evidence, see www.texas-midwife.com/breastfeeding.htm.

take this custom into consideration. A Levite child's duties began at age three (c.f. 2 Chron. 31:16); until then he was under the care of his mother. Similarly, Hannah turned her son Samuel over to tabernacle service "when she had weaned him" (1 Sam. 1:24); it is unlikely that she would have released an infant or a child of two to the care of the elderly priest Eli.

As a cultural commonplace, breastfeeding came readily to the mind of the sacred writers. Books in both the Old and New Testaments favor nursing and weaning as metaphors of God's care and His kingdom. For Isaiah, it is a metaphor for the abundance of the coming messianic age:

> You shall suck the milk of nations,
>   you shall suck the breast of kings;
> and you shall know that I, the LORD, am your Savior
>   and your Redeemer, the Mighty One of Jacob. (Is. 60:16)

In that day, prosperity will return to Jerusalem, which is portrayed, in Isaiah's final oracles, as a nursing mother to God's people:

> "Rejoice with Jerusalem, and be glad for her,
>   all you who love her;
> rejoice with her in joy,
>   all you who mourn over her;
> that you may suck and be satisfied
>   with her consoling breasts;
> that you may drink deeply with delight
>   from the abundance of her glory."
> For thus says the LORD:
> "Behold, I will extend prosperity to her like a river,
>   and the wealth of the nations like an overflowing stream;
> and you shall suck, you shall be carried upon her hip,
>   and dandled upon her knees.
> As one whom his mother comforts,
>   so I will comfort you;
>   you shall be comforted in Jerusalem." (Is. 66:10–13)

In the New Testament epistles, the apostles favor breastfeeding as the metaphor for spiritual formation, especially in its earliest stages. The apostle is like a nursing mother to the newly baptized, and his "milk" is the word of God. In his first letter, Saint Peter exhorts his readers and hearers: "Like newborn babes, long for the pure spiritual milk, that by it you may grow up to salvation" (1 Pet. 2:2). In a similar way, Saint Paul tells the Corinthians: "I fed you with milk, not solid food; for you were not ready for it" (1 Cor. 3:2). And the Letter to the Hebrews applies the metaphor to put arrogant Christians in their place:

> For though by this time you ought to be teachers, you need some one to teach you again the first principles of God's word. You need milk, not solid food; for every one who lives on milk is unskilled in the word of righteousness, for he is a child. (Heb. 5:12–13).

In both Testaments, mother's milk is a blessing. The curse is the "dry breasts." Yet, sometimes God's people deliberately choose the accursed way. In Lamentations, Jeremiah depicts this most vividly as a mother denying her child the milk of her breast:

> Even the jackals give the breast and suckle their young, but the daughter of my people has become cruel, like the ostriches in the wilderness. The tongue of the nursling cleaves to the roof of its mouth for thirst. (Lam. 4:3–4)

Indeed, Jesus saw those days of lamentation returning, a day when people would consider the greatest blessings of the covenant as curses, and the curse of dry breasts as a blessing: "For behold, the days are coming when they will say, 'Blessed are the barren, and the wombs that never bore, and the breasts that never gave suck!'" (Lk. 23:29). Luke surely intends these words of Jesus to evoke the blessing pronounced earlier in the Gospel by the anonymous woman in the crowd. Could there be any more vivid illustration of the contrast between blessing and curse?

Breastfeeding in the Fathers and Doctors

The earliest Christians lived in the same cultural milieu as their scriptural ancestors. Extended breastfeeding was the norm throughout the Mediterranean world; sometimes, especially among the upper classes, mothers delegated this duty to a wet nurse, a lactating woman who suckled children in the place of their mother. Some people did practice artificial feeding, but it was very rare; primitive methods and a poor understanding of sanitation made the practice extremely difficult and even hazardous.

The childhood world of the Fathers, then, was continuous with that of the Bible, and the Fathers eagerly took up the metaphors they found in the scriptural models. Moreover, they developed the metaphors, extending them not only to the relationship between God and humankind, but also to the relations among the divine Persons in the Trinity. In the pseudonymous "Odes of Solomon," Jewish-Christian poems of the late first or early second century, God compares himself to a nursing mother:

> For I turn not my face from my own, because I know them.
> And before they had existed I recognized them . . .
> I fashioned their members, and my own breasts I prepared for them,
> that they might drink my holy milk and live by it.[3]

In other Odes, the human narrator speaks of his sense of divine filiation in suckling terms:

> And I was carried like a child by its mother;
>   and He gave me milk, the dew of the Lord.
> And I was enriched by His favor, and rested in His perfection.[4]

The milk is a created participation in God's uncreated nature. It is a gift, and a grace, bestowed by the Holy Spirit. As the odist wrote:

---

[3] Ode 8:12–14 in James H. Charlesworth, ed. and trans., *Old Testament Pseudepigrapha*, vol. 2 (Princeton, N.J.: Princeton University, 1983). The origins and even orthodoxy of the Odes have been much disputed in recent years. One thing is certain: They exercised a powerful influence on the great Fathers of the Alexandrian and East Syrian schools.

[4] Ode 35:5–6.

The Holy Spirit opened Her bosom,
    and mixed the milk of the two breasts of the Father.
Then She gave the mixture to the generation without their knowing,
    and those who have received it are in the perfection of the
    right hand.[5]

At the end of the second century, Saint Clement of Alexandria develops these images still further, speaking of Christ as the "Word who is milk,"[6] milk of the Father, and of the Eucharist as the sacrament of this divine nourishment:

"Heavenly food is similar to milk in every way: by its nature it is palatable through grace; nourishing, for it is life; and dazzling white, for it is the light of Christ. Therefore, it is more than evident that the blood of Christ is milk."

In a long, poetic meditation, Clement preaches on salvation, comparing it at every step to the physiology of human lactation. He returns again and again to the notion of Christ as nourishing and as nourishment. The Father's "care-banishing breast" is Jesus, "the breast that is the Word, who is the only one who can truly bestow on us the milk of love. Only those who nurse at the breast are blessed."[7]

The imagery recurs frequently in the early Syriac Fathers as well, especially Saint Ephrem, a fourth-century doctor of the Church. Meditating on the Nativity, he wrote of Jesus:

He is the Breast of Life and the Breath of Life. . . .
When He sucked the breast of Mary,
    He was suckling all with His life.
While He was lying on His Mother's bosom,
    in His bosom were all creatures lying.[8]

[5] Ode 19:4–5.
[6] Clement of Alexandria, *Christ the Educator*, Simon P. Wood, C.P., ed. and trans., vol. 23 in Fathers of the Church (Washington: Catholic University of America, 1954), 35.
[7] Ibid., 41.
[8] Saint Ephrem, *Nativity Hymns* 3, ed. John Gwynn, in Nicene and Post-Nicene Fathers, series 2, vol. 13, part II (reprint, Peabody, Mass.: Hendrickson, 2004), 233.

In the same century, a Syriac manual of the spiritual life, the Book of Steps (*Liber Graduum*), praised the visible Church, which "with its altar and baptism—gives birth to people as infants, who suckle milk until they are weaned."[9]

The catena of breastfeeding images applied to God stretches from the Scriptures through the patristic era. Nor is it a peculiarity of Eastern Christianity. At the end of the second century, Saint Irenaeus of Lyons—who himself served as a great bridge between East and West—wrote that "we need to take refuge in the Church, to drink milk at her breast, to be fed with the Scriptures of the Lord."[10]

In fifth-century North Africa, Saint Augustine echoed the ancient thoughts of Clement and Ephrem. It was he who cried out to God: "what am I but a creature suckled on Your milk and feeding on You, the food that never perishes?"[11] And later in the same book he said: "For 'the Word was made flesh' in order that Your wisdom, by which You created all things, might become milk for our infancy."[12] Elsewhere he put it most simply: "Our milk is Christ," he said, fed to us from "Mother Church," whose "breasts are the two testaments of the divine Scriptures."[13]

The idea finds expressions in the mystics and doctors of the Church down through the ages. In the eighteenth century, Saint Alphonsus Liguori showed himself to be especially disposed to breastfeeding metaphors and imagery, speaking passionately of Jesus "in the Sacrament of the Altar," with His breasts all filled with milk; that is to say, with the graces, which, in His mercy, He desires to bestow upon us. And as a mother, whose breasts are overcharged with milk, goes about seeking for children who

---

[9] *Liber Graduum* 12.2. *The Book of Steps: The Syriac Liber Graduum*, trans. Robert A. Kitchen and Martien F.G. Parmentier (Kalamazoo, Mich.: Cistercian Publications, 2004), 121.

[10] Saint Irenaeus, *Against Heresies* 5.20.2, quoted in Olivier Clement, *The Roots of Christian Mysticism*, tr. Theodore Berkeley (London: New City Press, 1995), 96.

[11] Saint Augustine of Hippo, *Confessions* 4.1.1, in Penguin Classics, tr. R.S. Pine-Coffin (New York: Penguin, 1961), 71.

[12] *Confessions* 7.18.4.

[13] *Homilies on 1 John* 3.1, in Nicene and Post-Nicene Fathers, series 1, vol. 7 (reprint, Peabody, Mass.: Hendrickson, 2004), 476.

may draw it off and relieve her of its weight, so also does He call out to us, "You shall be carried at the breasts" (Is. 66:12, Douay-Rheims version).[14]

The Theology of the Body

The phrase, "theology of the body," has entered the common Catholic vocabulary relatively recently, with the teaching of Pope John Paul II. Yet, it is something we find implicit in these selected writings of the Church's Fathers and Doctors. The fundamental notion of this theological approach, according to Fathers Richard M. Hogan and John M. LeVoir, is this: "Interior spiritual realities reflect God; and when they are expressed through the body, it becomes a physical image of God in the world."[15]

Following after saints such as John Chrysostom,[16] Pope John Paul II has described the embodied love of man and woman—the conjugal act, with its ecstasy and fecundity—as an image of the inner life of the Trinitarian God. The Fathers saw no less in the act of breastfeeding. Thus, a nursing woman becomes a "physical image of God in the world": loving, provident, nourishing, teaching, saving, consoling, and care-banishing. A mother gives herself to her child as Christ gives Himself to every Christian in the Eucharist. And, for the nursing mother, as for Jesus, the giving is sacrificial. "God's parental tenderness can also be expressed by the image of motherhood," says the Catechism of the Catholic Church, "which emphasizes God's immanence, the intimacy between Creator and creature. The language of faith thus draws on human experience of parents, who are in a way the first representatives of God for man."[17]

---

[14] Saint Alphonsus Liguori, *Visits to the Most Blessed Sacrament and to the Blessed Virgin Mary*, ninth visit. Available online at www.praiseofglory.com/redemptorist/alphonsus. htm. See also his meditation "Jesus Taking Milk" in *The Incarnation, Birth, and Infancy of Jesus Christ* (Brooklyn: Redemptorist Fathers, 1927), 246ff.

[15] Richard M. Hogan and John M. LeVoir, *Covenant of Love* (San Francisco: Ignatius, 1992), 42.

[16] Saint John Chrysostom, *Homilies on Ephesians 20*, quoted in Scott Hahn and Mike Aquilina, *Living the Mysteries* (Huntington, Ind.: Our Sunday Visitor, 2003), 221–222.

[17] *Catechism of the Catholic Church*, n. 239. None of this can be made to justify goddess worship, or calling upon God as "Our Mother."

The nursing mother is an icon of God. This is true of every nursing mother, but especially of the Blessed Virgin Mary—for she was a sinless mother nourishing the incarnate Son of God. Thus, *Maria lactans* has always been a favored subject in Christian art.[18] In one of the earliest representations of the Madonna, in the Roman catacombs, she is portrayed with her suckling Child. The first Marian shrine built in the Americas was dedicated to Mary under the title *Nuestra Señora de la Leche y Buen Parto* (Our Lady of Plentiful Milk and a Good Delivery). And the museums declare the beauty of Mary's nursing motherhood in images by Leonardo, Michelangelo, Andrea de Solario, Van Eyck, Durer, Memling, El Greco, and many others.

These images are masterworks. But contemplation of a sacred icon is never merely or primarily an aesthetic experience. Every icon tells a story, and every image represents a moral universe. Pope John Paul II has used the theology of the body to examine the conjugal act as a sacred image, and he found there an implicit sexual morality. The sexual act is self-giving, life-giving, unifying, and fruitful—because God is. A good act, then, is one that is compatible with that divine image. An evil act is one that distorts the divine image, abuses it, defaces it, or renders it sterile.

The saints have taught us to find in the nursing couplet of mother and child a brilliant and vivid image of God. Only in recent centuries has the Church begun to discern the moral theology implicit in that image.

Breastfeeding and Creation

The work of the Church has been driven forward by developments in natural science and technology. It is not that modern Christians are the first to study breastfeeding scientifically. Clement of Alexandria studied the works of the ancient physicians in order to understand the physiology of human milk production. Saint

---

[18] See Helenka Varencov, "The Nursing Madonna: A Cultural Motif," in *The Nursing Mother: Historical Insights from Art and Theology* (Oak Park, Ill.: Child & Family Reprint Booklet Series, 1969).

Augustine began his autobiographical *Confessions* with a natural history of his own infancy.

> But neither my mother nor my nurses filled their breasts of their own accord, for it was you who used them, *as your law prescribes*, to give me infant's food and a share of the riches which you distribute even among the very humblest of all created things. It was also by your gift that I did not wish for more than you gave, and that my nurses gladly passed on to me what you gave to them. They did this because they loved me in the way *that you had ordained*, and their love made them anxious to give me what they had received in plenty from you. For it was to their own good that what was good for me should come to me from them; though, of course, it did not come to me from them but, through them, from you, because you, my God, are the source of all good.[19]

Here, Augustine describes nature's powerful convergence of physical, emotional, and spiritual forces. Creation obeys a "law" that God Himself has "ordained." One person's need determines another's duty. One woman's natural drive satisfies a little baby's inexorable need. Moreover, Augustine concluded that all these ordered elements of creation are signs of something still greater. They are signs that "proclaim the truth" of God's goodness. It is his imaginative recounting of himself as a suckling that elicits the *Confessions*' first meditation in praise of God's providence.

But Augustine really didn't know the half of it. Researchers are only now beginning to appreciate the component complexity of breast milk.

Beyond the proteins, minerals, vitamins, fats, and sugars needed for nourishment, there are antibodies in milk to help fend off infection during the early months, when the baby's own immune system is still too weak to work; growth factors thought to help in tissue development and maturation; and an abundance of hormones, neuropeptides, and natural optoids that may subtly shape the newborn's brain and behavior.[20]

---

[19] Saint Augustine, *Confessions* 1.6 in Pine-Coffin translation, emphasis added.
[20] Natalie Angier, "Mother's Milk Found to Be Potent Cocktail of Hormones," *New York Times*, May 24, 1994, p. C1.

To detail the patriarch Jacob's "blessings of the breast," a modern Christian woman might list the following:

- Breastfeeding reduces the mother's risk of hemorrhaging after birth.[21]
- Breastfeeding reduces the mother's risk of breast and uterine cancer.[22]
- Breastfeeding delays the return of fertility.[23]
- Breastfeeding produces prolactin and oxytocin, chemicals that relax women for the work of mothering.[24]

Such benefits should be enough to recommend the practice. But the blessings fall not only to mothers. Remember, the woman in Luke's Gospel could only guess at Mary's beatitude because of the great virtue of Mary's son, Jesus. What blessings does a child, like Jesus, gain through the experience of breastfeeding?

- Breastmilk provides antibodies to illnesses.[25]
- Breastmilk reduces the incidence of allergies.[26]
- Breastmilk has been linked to brain development and higher I.Q. scores.[27]

---

[21] Barbara Harper, R.N., *Gentle Birth Choices* (Rochester, Vt.: Healing Arts, 1994), 27.

[22] This is abundantly documented. See, e.g., S.Y. Lee et al., "Effect of Lactation on Breast Cancer Risk: A Korean Woman's Cohort Study," *International Journal of Cancer* 2003; 105(3): 390–393. Also: Collaborative Group on Hormonal Factors in Breast Milk, "Collaborative Reanalysis of Individual Data from 47 Epidemiological Studies," *Lancet* 2002; 360:187–195. Also: M. Helewa et al., "Breast Cancer, Pregnancy, and Breastfeeding," *Journal of Obstetrics and Gynaecology Canada* 2002; 24(2):165–171.

[23] Sheila Kippley, *Breastfeeding and Natural Child Spacing* (Cincinnati, Ohio: Couple to Couple League, 1999); also M. Labbok, "The Lactational Amenorrhea Method: Another Choice for Mothers," *Breastfeeding Abstracts* 1993; 13:3–4; and K. Kennedy and C. Visness, "Contraceptive Efficacy of Lactational Amenorrhoea," *Lancet* 1992; 339:227–30.

[24] See E. Sibolboro and E.S. Katki, "Breastfeeding Is Associated with Reduced Perceived Stress and Negative Mood in Mothers," *Health Psychology* 2002; 21(2): 187–193. Also: M. Heinrichs et al., "Lactation and Stress: Protective Effects of Breast-Feeding in Humans," *Stress* 2002; 5(3):195–203.

[25] See M.K. Davis, "Breastfeeding and Chronic Disease in Childhood and Adolescence," *Pediatric Clinics of North America* 2001; 48(1):125–141. Also: P.D. Scariati et al., "A Longitudinal Analysis of Infant Morbidity and the Extent of Breastfeeding in the United States," *Pediatrics* 1997; 99(6):e5.

[26] W.H. Oddy et al., "Maternal Asthma, Infant Feeding, and the Risk of Asthma in Childhood," *Journal of Allergy and Clinical Immunology* 2002; 110:65–67.

[27] See E.L. Mortensen, "The Association Between Duration of Breastfeeding and Adult Intelligence," *Journal of the American Medical Association* 2002; 28(15):2365–2371.

- Breastfeeding promotes proper development of jaw, teeth, and speech.[28]
- Breastfeeding keeps mother and baby close, building strong ties of love.
- Breastfed children are less likely to become obese adults.[29]

In 1941, Pope Pius XII spoke of the "mysterious influences" that pass between mother and child during breastfeeding. With time, and with advances in the medical arts and sciences, we are growing in our understanding of these mysteries of creation. We are learning, quite specifically, how blessed are the breasts that nurse—and how blessed is the child who nurses. The blessings start in the natural order and gradually ascend from there.

The Morals of Breastfeeding

The metaphors of breastfeeding were, for almost two millennia, a commonplace of Christian homiletics, poetry, and theology. If they seem unusual to us today, perhaps it is because we have suffered a disconnection from our ancestors—perhaps, more significantly, we have suffered a disconnection from nature. It is at least arguable that the maternal feeding of the young has been denatured by formula feeding.[30]

With modern methods of sanitation came safer methods of artificial feeding for children who were orphaned or otherwise separated from their mothers. With mass production, however, the baby bottle soon became a product in search of a market—sold as a fashionable modern convenience. Whereas formerly only the upper classes could hire a wet-nurse, now all

---

Also: "Long-Chain Polyunsaturated Fatty Acids in Human Milk and Brain Growth During Early Infancy," *Acta Pediatrica* 2000; 89(2):142–147.

[28] See the numerous medical studies catalogued in *The Womanly Art of Breastfeeding* (Schaumburg, Ill: La Leche League, 1997), 450–451.

[29] See, e.g., R. Locke, "Preventing Obesity: The Breast Milk-Leptin Connection," *Acta Paediatrica* 2002; 91(9):891–896.

[30] Herbert Ratner, M.D., drew an analogy between contraception and artificial feeding, but he attributed it to "some contraceptionists." "The Natural Institution of the Family" in *Nature, the Physician, and the Family: Selected Works of Herbert Ratner, M.D.*, ed. Mary Tim Baggott, M.D. (Bloomington, IN.: Author House, 2005), 207.

mothers could have the "freedom" to separate themselves from their smallest children.

No one would dispute the great good the baby bottle could do for orphans. But as large numbers of mothers opted for bottle-feeding instead of breastfeeding, some Catholic thinkers grew alarmed. In 1904, Bishop Denis Kelly of Ross, Ireland, wrote:

> If the clergy inquire, they will, I fear, be startled at the extent to which this primal duty of motherhood is at present violated. This is another serious cause of degeneration. I certainly think the clergy should instruct women on their moral obligation in this matter.[31]

Pope Pius XII issued perhaps the strongest and most authoritative statement of the matter:

> Many of the moral characteristics which you see in the youth or the man owe their origin to the manner and circumstances of his first upbringing in infancy . . . This is the reason why, except where quite impossible, it is more desirable that the mother should feed her child at her own breast.[32]

Pope John Paul II confirmed the moral weight of that passage by quoting it in his own "Address on Breastfeeding" in 1995. Since he was speaking to an audience far different from that of his predecessor—Pius was addressing mothers; John Paul, the Pontifical Academy of Sciences—he approached the problem in terms of the medical and psychological advantages of breastfeeding:

> In normal circumstances these include two major benefits to the child: protection against disease and proper nourishment. Moreover, in addition to these immunological and nutritional effects, this natural way of feeding can create a bond of love and

---

[31] Quoted in William D. Virtue, *Mother and Infant*, PhD dissertation (Rome: Pontifical University of Saint Thomas, 1995), 269.
[32] Pope Pius XII, "Allocution to Mothers," October 26, 1941. Reprinted in *L'Osservatore Romano*, May 24, 1995.

security between mother and child, and enable the child to assert
its presence as a person through interaction with the mother.[33]

Yet he returned to the same moral problem, asking whether
breastfeeding might represent "a vague utopia or *the obligatory
path to the genuine well-being of society*."[34] Pope John Paul II
did not answer the question directly, but called upon individuals,
societies, and institutions to develop family policies, so that
mothers receive the "time, information, and support" they need
in order to breastfeed successfully.

In the early 1990s, an American theologian, Father William
D. Virtue, produced a profound study of the moral issues sur-
rounding breastfeeding, *Mother and Infant: The Moral Theology
of Embodied Self-Giving in Motherhood in Light of the Exemplar
Couplet Mary and Jesus Christ*.[35] His book "starts with the needs
and rights of the human infant and reasons back to the duties of
the mother."[36] Father Virtue concluded:

> The natural law teaches that maternal breastfeeding is a norm of
> nature because of the physical and personal needs of the human
> infant which are uniquely met by breastmilk and attachment dur-
> ing nursing. This obligation is serious, but admits of parvity of
> matter if there is a serious reason to excuse and a sufficient alterna-
> tive is provided. The principal excuse for permitting bottle-feeding
> or a wet-nurse is inability, such as no milk; or necessity, such as the
> mother must work as sole support of the family.

The great Catholic philosopher of medicine Herbert Ratner
often approached the matter in terms of rights of the child. "Who
owns the milk?" he would ask. He argued that milk is one of the
few secretions that the human body produces not for the self, but
"for the sake of another." The child holds ownership of the milk,
and so has a right to receive it. According to Ratner, the child's
right corresponds to the mother's duty to breastfeed.

[33] Pope John Paul II, "Address on Breastfeeding," May 22, 1995, no. 2.
[34] Ibid., emphasis added.
[35] Virtue, op. cit.
[36] Ibid., p. 5.

The "Nursing Couplet" of Nazareth[37]

Blessed the breasts that nursed You. What was perfectly true of Mary and Jesus is surely true and capable of perfection in every nursing mother and child. The love that passed between Mary and her nursing baby, Jesus, is the love that God made possible for almost every mother and baby.[38]

The blessings of nursing are too many to count, and too mysterious to measure. We might say that breastfeeding has a "sacramental" quality; it stands as a natural sign of something divine. Indeed, it is among the most profound and personal experiences of the divine beauty revealed in nature. It is a light cast on Jesus' hidden infancy, and it is itself a revelation of God's providence and love.

Blessed the Breasts that Nursed You

Jesus replied to the woman: "Rather, blessed are they who hear the word of God and keep it."

Natural mothering alone was not what made the Virgin Mary blessed. She was blessed because she loved her son with a supernatural love as well. A devout Jew, a woman of prayer, she began every day by giving her whole heart and mind to God. This love she expressed in her deeds of love for others, most especially her child.

Blessed are they who hear the word of God and keep it. She always willed what was good for her baby, never putting her own wishes or comfort first. And so she nursed Him according to the cultural norm of her time. It is likely that she nursed Him for at least three years.

In this, she was blessed because she heard the word of God and kept it. From her *Magnificat*, the poem of praise she spoke to her cousin Elizabeth, we know that she was steeped in the

---

[37] For this phrase we are indebted, once again, to Herbert Ratner, M.D.. See his collection *The Nursing Couplet* (Oak Park, Ill.: Child & Family Reprint Booklet Series, 1988).

[38] Too late for discussion in this paper we received Sheila Kippley's *Breastfeeding and Catholic Motherhood: God's Plan for You and Your Baby* (Manchester, NH: Sophia Institute, 2005). This is a remarkable, deep, yet accessible work of spirituality.

revelation of the Holy Book and the promises of the covenant; her hymn is rich in allusions to the Hebrew Scriptures. The study of Scripture—with its praise of God's creation—surely made her attuned as well to God the Father's revelation in the book of nature. There, too, she discerned the will of God and kept it.

The goal of mothering for Mary of Nazareth, as for any woman today, is not only to raise a good child, but to also raise a good adult, someone who will know, love, and serve the Lord, and who will be fit for heaven at the end of a good earthly life.

What effect did nursing have upon Jesus at the end of His life? Only God knows. A clue could be found in His quotation of Psalm 22 in one of His last cries on the Cross: "My God, my God, why hast thou forsaken me?"

Through the centuries, so many have been scandalized by this line, because it seems to be an admission of despair. It is not. As Jesus suffered on the cross, His breaths were short and labored; He could speak but a few words at a time. Here, He gave us an abbreviated rendering of a Psalm that gave Him comfort. What does Psalm 22 say later on?

> Yet thou art he who took me from the womb;
>   thou didst keep me safe upon my mother's breasts.
> Upon thee was I cast from my birth,
>   and since my mother bore me thou hast been my God.
>   (Ps. 22:9–10)

His first human experiences were the same as almost any baby's can be, and they stayed with Him as His comfort to the end. Augustine prayed to the Virgin Mother: "Give milk, O mother, to him who is our food; give milk to the bread that comes down from heaven."[39]

Blessed the womb that bore you, the breasts that nursed you. Blessed is she who hears the word of God and keeps it.

---

[39] Saint Augustine, *Sermon* 369.1.

Discussion Questions

1. What does the act of breastfeeding signify about the God who created us?
2. Based on the evidence in the Bible and Fathers, how has society's perception of the female breast changed over the centuries? Is this a change for the better or worse?
3. How might Catholics help fulfill the papal calls for a society that supports breastfeeding mothers?
4. Who owns human breastmilk? What rights and duties follow from our answer to that question?

Terri Aquilina counsels breastfeeding women for La Leche League International. Mike is the author of many books on Catholic doctrine, devotion, and history and is co-host, with Scott Hahn, of several television series. They have been married for twenty years and have six children.

CHAPTER XIII

Adoption
Home Where You Belong

JEFF AND EMILY CAVINS

I n our personal life, there are two words that have radically changed our understanding of God in our day-to-day living: marriage and adoption. Both words speak of God's desire for intimacy with us and both point to the opportunity for us to reciprocate. Whether you are married, clergy or religious, or living a generous single life, an understanding of both marriage and adoption is crucial for understanding God and the meaning of life on earth. Through marriage, the two of us understood, in a deeper way, God's spousal relationship with the Church. And in having children, especially through adoption, we grew in appreciation of the familial bond of the Church. However, understanding these spousal and familial mysteries, which are rooted in the Trinity, is not to be limited to only those who have experienced marriage and children. All people can appreciate and experience these mysteries for we are all called to a spousal and familial relationship with God.

To become a child of God means to be adopted into His family. This is a powerful theological point, but for many people its impact is lost because of a misguided understanding of adoption.

One's first reaction to the word "adoption" is often to think that there was a problem that needed to be fixed, or we regard it lightly and joke about it: "Oh, he's the adopted one!" insinuating that the person is unlike the rest of the family, somehow different. In our society, the adopted person is often viewed as not quite a full member of the family. This mistaken view of adoption affects each one of us. Understanding what adoption truly means will lead us to a closer relationship with the Trinity and will help each person understand his or her own identity.

In our family, we have been blessed with three daughters. Our first was born after several years of struggling with infertility. Our younger two daughters came into our family through adoption. Until we went through the process, we did not have a full understanding of adoption, but the experience and the emotions taught us much and gave us a glimpse of the delight that God takes in his children.

When our oldest child was ten, we were living in Alabama in a modest home with an extra bedroom. Emily felt strongly about adding to our family, even though we had attempted to put the idea to rest after years of trying to have other children. However, our resignation to the idea of no more children did not dampen her desire to love. When Jeff saw Emily's genuine desire to love and nurture, we opened the doors anew to searching for children through adoption. We began talking to friends who had adopted, and, before we knew it, we were contacted by a friend about a young woman who was looking for a Catholic home for her soon-to-be-born infant girl. We were able to scrape up the funds, find a lawyer, and finish the home study in the eight weeks before the baby came.

During those exciting weeks the question came to mind: Could we love a second child *as much* as we loved our first child, Carly? This question is common to families who adopt. For us the answer to this question was "yes" from the very first moment we held our new child in our arms. The first words Jeff spoke to each of our girls as he first held them was: "I would die for you." The desire to love and protect them was instantaneous. There is absolutely no difference in how much these children are loved. All our girls are equally loved. Our love for the girls wasn't the result of anything that they did or didn't do, it was simply present in our hearts.

Another question that often arises in the minds of parents considering adoption is: Could we love an adopted child *in the same way* we would love a natural-born child? This question too was quickly answered for us. A bond of love was created even before the child was born, and the moment we saw her the bond was complete. That child is ours with no conditions, no comparisons, and no differences. No matter how many children you may be blessed with, each of them is loved with all of your love. It is no different if some, or all, of your children happen to be adopted. So it is with God. All of His children are equally loved and equally desired.

On the day we appeared in court to legally adopt our middle daughter, who had already been in our family for several months, the judge spoke clearly, echoing the words of Canon Law, "Children who have been adopted in accordance with the civil law are considered the children of that person or those persons who have adopted them" (Canon 110). That is how adoption works. The adoptee is forever a part of the new family.

How is it that we so often miss the deep meaning of adoption in the kingdom of God? The world's view of adoption centers around the notion of the "unwanted child," whereas the Kingdom of God centers around the "wanted child." The story of salvation is all about God in search of mankind, His wanted children. Each of us is a wanted child in God's family. The opportunity for Christian families to adopt is an extension of God's wish for children. Adoption is a real life example of how much God wants us. Our perspective is not that we are fixing a problem by adopting a child, rather we are celebrating a wonderful opportunity to love as God loves and to expand His family. Similarly, marriage mirrors God's plan for the union of Christ and His Church, so adoption mirrors God's plan to take all of us into His family. Our "yes" to our two adopted daughters was deeply rooted in God's "yes" for us. We knew that the adoption process we were a part of was rooted in Christ two thousand years ago. The Catechism points to the virginal conception of Christ as the beginning of God's worldwide adoption program (CCC 505). The choice and the accompanying emotions to expand our family was the result of our having been created in the image and likeness of God. Furthermore, our actions were a continuation of God ushering "in *the new birth* of children adopted in the Holy Spirit through faith" (CCC 505, emphasis in the original).

Just as our adoptive filiation with Christ gained us a real share in the life of the Trinity (CCC 654), so also our children's adoptive filiation with us gains for the child the riches of our family. Indeed, adoption is the means whereby we participate in the life of God's family.

Part of the participation in the life of the Trinity is the very desire for children. We see this heart-felt yearning for children in Hannah, who experienced a great desire to have a child. She told the Lord that, if she received a child from Him, she would give him back to the Lord all the days of his life (1 Sam. 1:11–13). One great benefit of adopting is the joy and fruit of parenting. It is an opportunity to take a child and present him or her to God. The ultimate goal of adoption is to love and nurture with the hope that the child will attain the beatific vision. Less than this misses the point.

The vocation of parenting is not simply a biological endeavor, but the responsibility to image the Trinity to children. Pope John Paul II said in *Familiaris Consortio:*

> The family is the first and fundamental school of social living: As a community of love, it finds in self-giving the law that guides it and makes it grow. The self-giving that inspires the love of husband and wife for each other is the model and norm for the self-giving that must be practiced in the relationships between brothers and sisters and the different generations living together in the family. (no. 37)

A father's and mother's love is not impeded by the child's color, size, or physical ability. Every child is created in the image of God and therein lays his or her value. If these concepts were understood, pregnant mothers in difficult circumstances would be more willing to carry their children to term because of available loving families. Rather than doubting that someone else could love and raise the children, the birthmothers could be part of the process to help their children get to heaven through the love of an adoptive family. In this way, the birthmother is not "giving up" the child, rather she is making a wise choice for the eternal life of the child. The birthmother can still be spiritually involved by praying for the eternal salvation of the child.

Sometimes when people learn that our children are adopted, we get the comment, "Oh, that was such a nice thing to do!" Though intended as well-meaning, the comment shows a mis-understanding regarding adoption. It was not for charity that we chose adoption. We chose adoption for our benefit, to add to our family, and to have more people to love and nurture. It is a natural desire to have a family, but through Christ adoption is raised to a supernatural desire.

God intends for us to live in families, so it is no surprise that family is what people value most in their relationships. Oftentimes people will remark after a natural disaster, "Though we lost all our belongings, we still have each other." This need for family is at the very core of the human person. John 13:34–35 exhorts us to love one another. We are loved by God and we are to love. God puts us in a family to learn love and to give love. It is the opportunity for each of us to mirror God's love for us to one another.

Issues of identity are common to all children as they grow. Often this is an issue for adopted children: to know where they came from, who they look like, what were the circumstances that brought them into the world. Their search for identity can be more visible than natural-born children, but ultimately, all children want to know who they are. Each child searches for that answer. The answer to our identity is finding our Father

in Heaven, through His son Jesus Christ. When we know our
purpose, we can identify who we are.

Genesis 1:26 tells us God has created each of us in His image.
His image as Trinity and eternal love are the foundation of who
we are. The Catechism of the Catholic Church defines this in
article 257:

> "O blessed light, O Trinity and first Unity!" God is eternal bless-
> edness, undying life, unfading light. God is love: Father, Son and
> Holy Spirit. God freely wills to communicate the glory of his
> blessed life. Such is the "plan of his loving kindness," conceived
> by the Father before the foundation of the world, in his beloved
> Son: "He destines us in love to be his sons" and "to be conformed
> to the image of his Son," through "the spirit of sonship." This
> plan is a "grace [which] was given to us in Christ Jesus before
> the ages began," stemming immediately from Trinitarian love. It
> unfolds in the work of creation, the whole history of salvation
> after the fall, and the missions of the Son and the Spirit, which
> are continued in the mission of the Church.

Throughout Scripture God reveals Himself in many ways. We
see Him as a shepherd in Psalm 23. We see Him as a husband in
the book of Hosea. God reveals Himself in how He takes care
of us. The Church teaches that:

> God is the *Father* Almighty, whose fatherhood and power shed
> light on one another: God reveals his fatherly omnipotence by
> the way he takes care of our needs; by the filial adoption that he
> gives us ("I will be a father to you, and you shall be my sons and
> daughters, says the Lord Almighty" [2 Cor. 6:18]). (CCC 270,
> emphasis in the original)

God reveals Himself to us as a father because that is our
greatest need.

In the Old Testament, God focuses on His first-born son,
Israel. Exodus 4:22 says, "And you shall say to Pharaoh, 'Thus
says the Lord, Israel is my first-born son.'" He establishes His
covenant with the children of Israel. God is trying to show the
Israelites who He is through His constant attention, care, instruction, discipline, and mercy.

As the plan of salvation unfolds, God brings as many people into His family as are willing to come. The very first paragraph of the *Catechism of the Catholic Church* explains this wonderful truth.

> God, infinitely perfect and blessed in himself, in a plan of sheer goodness freely created man to make him share in his own blessed life. For this reason, at every time and in every place, God draws close to man. He calls man to seek him, to know him, to love him with all his strength. He calls together all men, scattered and divided by sin, into the unity of his family, the Church. To accomplish this, when the fullness of time had come, God sent his Son as Redeemer and Savior. In his Son and through him, he invites men to become, in the Holy Spirit, his adopted children and thus heirs of his blessed life. (CCC 1)

God delights in the abundance of children, so much so that His suffering ushered in many sons to glory (Heb 2:10). The mission of the Trinity is manifested in adopted sons and daughters of God (CCC 690). When we understand that we are adopted in to God's family, it changes the way we interact with the world. We see others as potential sons and daughters of the Father. That was part of our reason for wanting to adopt children, so we could bring them to Jesus as we did on the day of their baptisms and continue to do each day through prayer and example.

Baptism is the avenue to entering God's family. We are adopted into God's family through baptism. "Baptism not only purifies from all sins, but also makes the neophyte 'a new creature,' an adopted son of God, who has become a 'partaker of the divine nature,' member of Christ and co-heir with him, and a temple of the Holy Spirit" (CCC 1265). Each member of the Church of Christ has been adopted by God to be His son or daughter. Not only are we created in the image of God, God has invited us through adoption into a setting by which we can further understand who we are and who God is. Baptism is an initiation into that realization.

The term adoption is used by Paul to describe our new relationship with God in Romans 8:13–17.

For if you live according to the flesh you will die, but if by the
Spirit you put to death the deeds of the body you will live. For
all who are led by the Spirit of God are sons of God. For you
did not receive the spirit of slavery to fall back into fear, but you
have received the spirit of sonship. When we cry, "Abba! Father!"
it is the Spirit himself bearing witness with our spirit that we are
children of God, and if children, then heirs, heirs of God, and
fellow heirs with Christ, provided we suffer with him in order
that we may also be glorified with him.

Paul writes within the context of the Roman laws of the
day that governed adoption. Roman adoptions were subject to
patria potestas, the father's power over his family, which was
the power of absolute disposal and control. Adoption in Roman
times took place in two steps. First, three times the birth father
symbolically sold his son, with the first two times buying him
back and the third time not buying him back, thereby breaking
the *patria potestas.* Secondly, the adopting father went to the
Roman magistrates and presented a legal case for the transfer-
ence of the person to be adopted into his *patria potestas.* When
all this was completed, the adoption was final. Thereafter, the
adopted person lost all rights in his old family and gained all the
rights of a legitimate son in his new family. In the most binding
way, he received a new father. He then became heir to his new
father's estate. Even if other sons were born to his father after his
adoption, it did not affect his rights. He was co-heir with them.
By law, the old life of the person was completely wiped out; all
debts were cancelled. He was regarded as a new person entering
into a new life. In the eyes of the law, he was absolutely the son
of his new father.

Paul says that God's Spirit witnesses with our spirit that we
really are His children (see Rom. 8:16–17). In ancient times, the
adoption ceremony was carried out in the presence of seven witnesses who swore that the adoption was legitimate. In this way,
the right of the adopted person was guaranteed and he entered
into his inheritance. Paul is saying that the Holy Spirit Himself is
the witness to our adoption into the family of God.

This means for us that we were once in absolute control of our sinful human nature, but God in His mercy has brought us into His absolute possession. The old life has no more rights over us; God now has absolute right. The past is cancelled and we begin a new life with God and become heirs of all His riches. In short, we are joint-heirs with Jesus Christ. That which Christ inherits, we also inherit. If Jesus has to suffer, we also inherit that suffering; but if Christ was raised to life, we too will be raised to life eternal.

Through baptism, God has adopted us all into His family. This was the plan from the beginning. John 1:12 tells us: "But to all who receive him, who believed in his name, he gave power to become children of God." To aid us in our new life in God's family, the Church provides us with many sacraments and instructions in the ways of God.

The process of God adopting us rests in the free act of God. Adoption's purpose is for us to enjoy God and live in divine sonship. The whole idea of adoption or divine sonship is set forth by Saint Paul in such a way that one may see that the new relationship toward the Father is diametrically opposed to the spirit of bondage (Romans 8:15).

If you are considering adoption, realize that the love of God cannot only change your life but the lives of children brought into your household. God's grace will be there. After a men's conference in which Jeff shared his journey of adopting children, we received a call from a man who admitted he had been living a selfish lifestyle, which did not include children, although his wife wanted to raise a family. The outcome of this man's conversion of heart, after understanding how much God wants us and how much we are to mirror God, was the adoption of a sibling group of four children. They graciously invited us to the baptism of all four of them. What an inspiring testimony of God's love when we learned of this expanded family. It is not uncommon for the husband to pause at the idea of adding more children to the family, whereas the wife has the natural desire to nurture children. One of the best ways a husband can show love to his wife is to be open to children, either naturally or through adoption.

Adoption changes our whole understanding of God as we come face to face with His love for us. At the same time, it kindles the desire in our hearts to pour ourselves out for others. As parents who have adopted children, we are simply acting out what has been done for us by God. Through adoption we have come to understand it is more blessed to give than to receive.

Discussion Questions

1. What has been your view of adoption? How has this chapter shed light on what adoption means in the scope of the family of God?

2. Discuss the correlation between living in a human family and living in the family of God. What needs do they meet? What role does identity play?

3. How do we know that we are part of the family of God? What evidence is there from Rom. 8:16–17 and CCC 1265?

4. How does the realization that you are adopted by God change your view of family relationships?

Jeff Cavins is an editor and writer of Catholic Scripture Study. He is also co-editor of Ascension Press' Amazing Grace *book series, as well as a contributing author for the* Catholic for a Reason *series. He also has developed an interactive Bible timeline system,* The Great Adventure: A Journey through the Bible.

Jeff and Emily reside in Minnesota with their three daughters, Carly, Jacqueline, and Antonia.

Appendix I

Liturgy for the Dedication of the Home as a Miniature Church, and for the Installation of the Father and Mother as Its Pastor and Associate

Priest: Dear members and friends of this household:

It is an ancient and constant teaching of Holy Church that those who receive Baptism in the Church receive a priestly character which, though essentially different in kind from the character given in ordination to the sacramental priesthood, is nevertheless real and of deep significance.

It is also the teaching of the Church that the Catholic Christian family is intended by God to be of such a nature as to deserve to be called a "little Church"; that all baptized members of each family household are to exercise there, in appropriate ways, the priesthood conferred on them in baptism; and that the father is, by divine institution, appointed as chief pastor of this "little Church," and his wife is appointed here, as elsewhere, to be his helpmate, as Pope John XXIII taught in his encyclical, "Near the Chair of Peter" on June 29, 1959:

> Let the father of the family take the place of God among his children, and not only by his authority but by the upright example of his life also stand clearly in the first place. Let the mother, however, rule firmly over her offspring by gentleness and virtue in the domestic setting. Let her behave with indulgence and love towards her husband and, along with him, let her carefully instruct and train her family.

All this being so, dear friends, we are gathered together here today under the patronage of the Holy Virgin Mary, Mother of God and of the Church, and Saint Joseph, head of the Holy Family and Patron of the Universal Church, to call down God's blessing on this household, to establish it as a "little Church" in which He may deign to dwell, and to install the father of the family as its pastor, and the mother as his divinely appointed assistant and loving counselor, so that it may become firmly established on the faith, and be the center of a widely radiating charity, grounded in a loving obedience to the Vicar of Christ and all bishops in union with him.

Blessing of a Home as a Little Church and Installation of the Father as Its Pastor

Verse: Peace to this house;

Response: And to all who live in it.

V: My house shall be called a house of prayer, says the Lord (cf. Mt. 21:13);

R: Like living stones let us be built on Christ as a spiritual house, a holy priesthood (cf. 1 Pet. 2:5).

V: You are the temple of God, and God's Spirit dwells in you. The temple of God is holy; you are that temple.

R: Can it be indeed that God dwells among men on earth? Greatly to be feared is God in His sanctuary. He, the God of Israel, gives power and strength to His people. Blessed be God!

Prayer: Look kindly on the prayer and petition of your servants, O Lord our God. May Your eyes watch night and day over this temple, where You have decreed You shall be honored. Listen to the petitions of Your servants which they offer in this earthly dwelling of Yours. Listen from Your heavenly dwelling and grant pardon and peace, to the praise and glory of Your Name, for the good of our household and of all Your Church.

R. Amen.

Ant.: *Unless the Lord build the house*
they labor in vain who build it. (Ps. 127)
Blessed are all they that fear the Lord . . .
    blessed are you and it shall be well with you;
Ant.:
Your wife shall be as a fruitful vine
    on the walls of your house;
Your children as olive plants
    round about your table . . .

Ant.:

May the Lord bless you out of Sion
    and may you see the good things of Jerusalem
    all the days of your life;
May you see your children's children
    and peace upon Israel. (Ps. 128)

Ant.:

Prayer: Father, who makes Your Church on earth a sign of the new and eternal Jerusalem, send Your Holy Spirit upon this dwelling that it may become a temple of Your presence and a home of Your glory, through Jesus Christ, Your Son, our Lord, who lives and reigns with You and the same Holy Spirit, one God, world without end.

R: Amen.

Priest: Whose household is this?

Husband and wife: It is ours.

Priest: Hear, Father of this house, appointed by God to rule with authority, and hear, Mother of this house, appointed by God to preside in love: The Lord is our God, the Lord alone! Therefore you shall love the Lord your God with all your heart, and with all your soul, and with all your strength. Take to heart these words which I enjoin on you today. Drill them into your children. Speak of them at home and abroad, whether you are busy or at rest. (cf. Deut. 6:4–7)

Father: One thing I ask of the Lord, this I seek: to dwell in the house of the Lord all the days of my life.

Mother: That I may gaze on the loveliness of the Lord and contemplate his temple.

Father: Your Presence, O Lord, I seek. Hide not your face from me;

Mother: I believe that I shall see the bounty of the Lord in the land of the living.

All: Father, make them holy in the truth. As you sent me into the world, I have sent them into the world. (cf Jn. 17:17–18)

Priest: I have found David my servant;
    with my holy oil I have anointed him,

That my hand may be always with him,
and that my arm may make him strong.
(cf. Ps. 89: 20–21)

Father, accept and sanctify the holy purposes of these Your servants, N and N. By Your grace they have dedicated to You today this dwelling and all who live in it, to be a dwelling also for the Most Holy Trinity. Help them to serve You always in this "little Church." You have entrusted to their authority and love, to raise their children in the fear and love of Your Name, and to be a united witness, within Your Church Universal, to the new and eternal life won by Christ's redemption. Grant these prayers through Jesus Christ Your Son, our Lord, who lives and reigns with You in the unity of the Holy Spirit, One God, world without end.

R: Amen.

Solemn Blessing

Priest: God our Father made you children by water and the Holy Spirit: may He bless you and watch over you with His fatherly love.

R: Amen.

Priest: Jesus Christ the Son of God promised that the Spirit of truth would be with His Church forever: may He bless you and give you courage in professing the true faith.

R: Amen.

Priest: The Holy Spirit came down upon the disciples and set their hearts on fire with love: may He bless you, keep you one in faith and love, and bring you to the joy of God's kingdom.

R: Amen.

Priest: May almighty God bless you, the Father,
and the Son, + and the Holy Spirit.

R: Amen.

Appendix II

Family Sacred Heart Enthronement Liturgy[1]

How to Prepare the "Throne"

A fireplace mantel is ideal for the "throne:" or a table may be arranged like an altar with a white cloth, candles, and flowers. In another part of the room, or in a separate room, there will be needed a table on which to place the Sacred Heart image and the family Bible before the ceremony. The ceremony will begin at this table, or dining room table.

Note: If a picture is used, in order to bring out the idea of a shrine, a wall bracket for flowers and candles may be erected below the picture. Have picture/statue blessed in advance.[2]

How to Prepare Spiritually

If possible, receive Communion on the Day of Enthronement or on the previous Sunday for blessings of the Sacred Heart on the family.

For three days prior to ceremony say the rosary (as family or individually).

Preliminary Explanation

(All are *seated* while the father—or in his absence, mother, or another—explains what is about to take place.)

Father: You know I think this might well be one of the most important gatherings of our life. I say this because I'm convinced from what we have been told and what I've read about the

---

[1] This liturgy is provided here by permission of the National Enthronement Center, P.O. Box 111, Fairhaven, MA 02719-0111.

[2] This ritual may also be used when a priest presides, which is highly recommended. In this case he acts as a witness. After the reading of the Gospel (see no. 2), he gives a homily applying it to the family, and reminding them of Jesus' love for the family. He may bless the picture/statue as part of the liturgy. See no. 13 below.

Enthronement that it brings terrific blessings to families. And the good Lord knows we need them.

By the Enthronement, we are told, we proclaim Jesus as our King who rules over us through love—more like a Father than a ruler. He becomes our generous Provider, our family Friend, our spiritual Physician, our constant Companion, the unseen Guest at every meal.

And we want Him to be all these things because each and every one of us needs His help. It isn't easy to be good. We can't do it alone, but with Jesus' help we can make it.

Now let us all stand.

1. Penitential Rite

Father: The home is a "little church." The Enthronement is our family liturgy, or family worship. In our parish church we prepare ourselves for Mass by expressing sorrow for our sins. So here, in this "domestic" church, we begin our family liturgy by telling God we are sorry for the faults we have committed in our daily family life, especially those against charity.

Let us pause for a moment and recall the times we have offended God by hurting one another *(pause)*. Let us tell Him we are sorry and ask His forgiveness.

Father: Loving Father, You sent Your Son Jesus into the world to give us an example of true Christian family life. Forgive us for the many times we have forgotten Jesus in our family life: Lord have mercy.

All: Lord have mercy.

Mother: Sacred Heart of Jesus, forgive us for our neglect of family prayer, especially the family Rosary: Christ have mercy.

All: Christ have mercy.

Children (or Leader): Holy Spirit, Spirit of Love, we have offended You by failing to love one another and our neighbor: Lord have mercy.

All: Lord have mercy.

All: May Almighty God have mercy on us, forgive us our sins, and bring us to life everlasting. Amen.

Father: Let us now listen to Jesus telling each of us how much He loves us. Notice well that He does not call us servants, but *friends*.

2. The Word of God

Reader: The Lord be with you.

All: And also with you.

Reader: A reading from the Holy Gospel according to John.

All: Glory to You, O Lord.

Reader: As the Father has loved me, so I have loved you. Live on in my love. You will live in my love if you keep my commandments, even as I have kept my Father's commandments, and live in His love. All this I tell you that your joy may be complete. This is my commandment: Love one another as I have loved you. There is no greater love than this: to lay down one's life for one's friends. You are my friends if you do what I command you.

I no longer speak to you as servants, for a servant does not know what his master is about. Instead, I call you friends since I have made known to you all that I have heard from my Father.

It is not you who chose me, it was I who chose you to go forth and bear fruit. Your fruit must endure, so that all you ask the Father in my name He will give you. The command I give you is this that you love one another. (Jn.15:9–17)

This is the Gospel of the Lord.

All: Praise to you, Lord Jesus Christ.[3]

3. The Enthronement Ceremony

Father: Now, in Your name, I enthrone the Sacred Heart as the Head of our family.

(All gather around the father, who takes the Sacred Heart image, and mother, who takes the Bible[4] and slowly walks to the place prepared for the Enthronement. There he places the image of Jesus on the throne; then mother places the Bible next to it.)

---

[3] If a priest is present, he may give a homily. He then blesses the picture (see no. 13).

[4] The Bible: Reading Sacred Scripture should become an integral part of family prayer life. "Learn to know the Heart of God in the Word of God" (Saint Gregory the Great).

All: Jesus, You are the King and Friend of our family. We accept Your loving rule over us. Stay with us as our best Friend. We need You.

Father: Now let us pray the Apostles' Creed as an act of faith and reparation.

4. The Apostles' Creed

I believe in God, the Father Almighty, Creator of heaven and earth; and in Jesus Christ, His only Son, our Lord, who was conceived by the Holy Spirit, born of the Virgin Mary, suffered under Pontius Pilate, was crucified, died and was buried. He descended into hell; the third day He rose again from the dead; He ascended into heaven, sits at the right hand of God, the Father Almighty; from there He shall come to judge the living and the dead. I believe in the Holy Spirit, the Holy Catholic Church, the communion of saints, the forgiveness of sins, the resurrection of the body, and life everlasting. Amen.

5. Father: Today we are going to turn our family over to the Sacred Heart of Jesus. When we were baptized we were dedicated to God. That's what we are going to do now—renew our dedication by consecrating ourselves to His loving Heart. This is our Family Covenant with God. Let us all kneel.

6. Father: Almighty and Eternal Father, we, the . . . *(family name)* . . . family,

(Note: At this time, each member of the family speaks his/her first name, beginning with the father. Absent members may be named.)

(Now all continue together. . .) consecrate ourselves and our home to the Sacred Heart of Your only begotten Son, Jesus Christ, Our Lord, who loves us with a tender and everlasting love. May we return this love as He comes into the midst of our family to live and share our life in a special way from this day on.

We freely choose to make this covenant of love with You, Father, and dedicate to the Heart of Jesus all that we have, without any reservation on our part, promising to amend our lives by turning from sin and all that might lead us into sin.

Jesus, we accept You as a living member of our family. Sanctify our joys and comfort us in our sorrows. May Your Holy Spirit continually make us aware of Your special presence among us, and in one another.

Stay with us, Lord, and through this consecration help us to have a deep and loving respect for one another. Help us to imitate Your gentle and humble Heart, that we may give ourselves to each other by the faithful performance of our family obligations.

With the motherly aid of the Immaculate Heart of Mary, may this Enthronement of Your living, loving Heart, Your divine and glorified Heart, O Jesus, lead us to a renewed confidence in Your merciful love, for each of us individually and, at the same time, for all families, especially the poor and the oppressed.

Use us, Lord, to make Your love known beyond our home. Dispel all our doubts. Strengthen our faith. Fill us with holy hope. Guide us to the solutions necessary to bring about justice and peace for all. Wipe away our fears and anxieties. Teach us to use properly all material goods at our disposal. Show us the way to overcome class hatred and civil strife. Penetrate us with Your love, for it is in doing Your holy will that we desire to find our way to Your Father. Amen.

Sacred Heart of Jesus, we love You. Sacred Heart of Jesus, Thy Kingdom come! Immaculate Heart of Mary, pray for us. Saint Joseph, pray for us. Saint Margaret Mary, pray for us. Glory to the Sacred Hearts of Jesus and Mary for ever and ever. Amen.

7. General Intercessions (stand)

Father: That the Sacred Heart of Jesus may be known, loved and served in a special way, in our home, in our neighborhood, and in our parish, we pray to the Lord.

All: Lord, hear our prayer.

Mother: That Mary, our Mother, through her Immaculate Heart may help us keep alive the spirit of our Enthronement, by bringing us together daily to pray in the name of Jesus, let us pray to the Lord.

All: Lord, hear our prayer.

Children (or Parents): For all the members of our family who are not with us today, both living and dead, let us pray to the Lord;

All: Lord, hear our prayer.

All: That God may bless all bishops, priests, and religious and grant an increase of vocations to the priesthood and religious life, let us pray to the Lord.

All: Lord, hear our prayer.

(Note: Personal requests may be added, if desired.)

8. Litany of Thanksgiving

Father: Just as we thank God, our heavenly Father, through Jesus, His Son, during the Mass, so also now we thank the Sacred Heart of Jesus through the Immaculate Heart of His Mother.

Mother: For giving us our children.

All: We thank You, Lord.

Children: For giving us our parents.

All: We thank You, Lord.

Father: For coming to our home.

All: We thank You, Lord.

Mother: For giving us Mary, Your Mother, as our Mother.

All: We thank You, Lord.

Father: For the gift of faith and for all the blessings and joys of our past family life.

All: We thank You, Lord.

9. Father: Jesus is our King. Mary, His Mother, is our Queen. Many Catholics, by their sins, their bad talk, their immodesty, offend the Immaculate Heart of our Queen. As an act of reparation and to obtain her help, let us consecrate ourselves to her Immaculate Heart:

Queen of the Most Holy Rosary, and tender Mother of men, to fulfill the desires of the Sacred Heart, and the request of the

Vicar of your Son on earth, we consecrate ourselves to you and to your Immaculate Heart, and recommend to you all the families of our nation and of all the world.

Make our hearts and homes your shrine, and through us make the Heart of Jesus rule and triumph in every family in the world. Amen.

10. The parents now give their children the parental blessing. The children *kneel* before the parents. First the father, then the mother, makes a sign of the Cross on the forehead of each child saying: "I bless you, my child, in the name of the Father, and of the Son, and of the Holy Spirit." The child answers, "Amen."

If a priest is present, he now blesses the family.

11. All sign the Enthronement Covenant (certificate): First, the father, then mother, followed by the children. The document should be framed and hung near the image of the Sacred Heart.

12. In honor of the divine King, Provider, Friend and Brother, refreshments may now be served.

13. Blessing of the Sacred Heart Image (This blessing is used if a priest is present. It should occur before no. 3 above)
Priest: Our help is in the name of the Lord.
All: Who made heaven and earth.
Priest: The Lord be with you.
All: And also with you.
Priest: Let us pray: Almighty everlasting God, Who approves the painting and sculpturing of the images of Your saints, so that as often as we gaze upon them we are reminded to imitate their deeds and sanctity: in Your kindness we implore You to bless + and sanctify + this image made in honor and in memory of the most Sacred Heart of Your only begotten Son, our Lord Jesus Christ; and grant that whosoever in its presence humbly strives to serve and honor the Sacred Heart of Your only begotten Son,

may obtain through His merits and intercession grace in this life and everlasting glory in the world to come. Amen.

The priest here sprinkles the image with Holy Water.

Important

To keep Jesus in your home and to make your family a "domestic church," pray together. "Where two or three are gathered in My name, I am there in their midst" (Mt. 18:20). To stay together, pray together.

The best time to renew your consecration might be before or after the evening meal. The following prayer is suggested, or, you may wish to compose your own. The important thing is to *pray,* as a *family,* especially the Rosary.

Daily Renewal of our Pledge

Dear Sacred Heart of Jesus, we renew our pledge of love and loyalty to You. Keep us always close to Your loving Heart, and to the most pure Heart of Your Mother.

May we love one another more and more each day, forgiving each other's faults as You forgive us our sins. Teach us to see You in the members of our family and those we meet outside our home, loving them as You love them, especially the poor and the oppressed, that we may be instrumental in bringing about justice and peace.

Please help us to carry our cross daily out of love for You, and to strengthen this love by frequent Mass and Communion.

Thank You, dear Jesus, King and Friend of our family, for all the blessings of this day. Protect us and all families during this night. Help us so to live that we may all get to Heaven.

Immaculate Heart of Mary, pray for us!

Saint Joseph, Protector of the Christian, pray for us!

Our Guardian Angels and Patron Saints, pray for us!

Bibliography

Abad, Javier and E. Fenoy. *Marriage: A Path To Sanctity.* Second Edition. New York: Scepter, 1988.

Aquilina, Mike. *The Mass of the Early Christians.* Huntington, IN: Our Sunday Visitor, 2001.

————. *The Way of the Fathers: Praying With the Early Christians.* Huntington, IN: Our Sunday Visitor, 1999.

Aquilina, Mike and Regis Flaherty. *The How-To Book of Catholic Devotions: Everything You Need to Know but No One Ever Taught You.* Huntington, IN: Our Sunday Visitor, 2000.

Burke, Cormac. *Covenanted Happiness: Love and Commitment in Marriage.* New York: Scepter, 1999.

Catechism of the Catholic Church. Second Edition. Washington, DC: United States Catholic Conference, Inc.—Libreria Editrice Vaticana, 1997.

Catholic for a Reason: Scripture and the Mystery of the Family of God. Edited by Scott Hahn and Leon Suprenant. Steubenville, OH: Emmaus Road, 1998.

Catholic for a Reason II: Scripture and the Mystery of the Mother of God. Second Edition. Edited by Scott Hahn and Leon Suprenant. Steubenville, OH: Emmaus Road, 2004.

Catholic for a Reason III: Scripture and the Mystery of the Mass. Edited by Scott Hahn and Regis J. Flaherty. Steubenville, OH: Emmaus Road, 2004.

Cavins, Jeff and Matt Pinto. *Amazing Grace for the Catholic Heart.* West Chester, PA: Ascension Press, 2003.

————. *Amazing Grace for Fathers.* West Chester, PA: Ascension Press, 2006.

————. *Amazing Grace for Married Couples.* West Chester, PA: Ascension Press, 2005.

————. *Amazing Grace for Mothers.* West Chester, PA: Ascension Press, 2004.

————. *Amazing Grace for Those Who Suffer.* West Chester, PA: Ascension Press, 2002.

Chesterton, G.K. *Brave New Family*. San Francisco: Ignatius Press, 1990.

Compendium of the Catechism of the Catholic Church. Washington, DC: United States Catholic Conference, Inc. —Libreria Editrice Vaticana, 2006.

Flaherty, Regis J. *Catholic Customs: A Fresh Look at Traditional Practices*. Cincinnati, OH: Servant, 2003.

————. *Last Things First*. Huntington, IN: Our Sunday Visitor, 2005.

Gray, Tim. *Sacraments in Scripture: Salvation History Made Present*. Steubenville, OH: Emmaus Road, 2001.

Gray, Tim and Curtis Martin. *Boys to Men: The Transforming Power of Virtue*. Steubenville, OH: Emmaus Road, 2001.

Hahn, Kimberly and Mary Hasson. *Catholic Education: Homeward Bound: A Useful Guide to Catholic Home Schooling*. San Francisco: Ignatius Press, 1996.

Hahn, Kimberly and Scott Hahn. *Life-Giving Love: Embracing God's Beautiful Design for Marriage*. Cincinnati, OH: Servant Books, 2001.

Hahn, Scott. *A Father Who Keeps His Promises: God's Covenant Love in Scripture*. Cincinnati, OH: Servant Books, 1998.

————. *First Comes Love: Finding Your Family in the Church and the Trinity*. New York: Doubleday, 2002.

————. *Lord, Have Mercy: The Healing Power of Confession*. New York: Doubleday, 2003.

————. *Swear to God: The Promise and Power of the Sacraments*. New York: Doubleday, 2004.

————. *The Lamb's Supper: The Mass as Heaven on Earth*. New York: Doubleday, 1999.

————. *Understanding "Our Father": Biblical Reflections on the Lord's Prayer*. Steubenville, OH: Emmaus Road, 2002.

Hahn, Scott, and Curtis Mitch. *Ignatius Catholic Study Bible*. Multiple volumes. San Francisco: Ignatius Press.

Hahn, Scott, and Mike Aquilina. *Living the Mysteries: A Guide for Unfinished Christians*. Huntington, IN: Our Sunday Visitor, 2003.

Healy, Mary. *Men and Women Are From Eden: A Study Guide to John Paul II's Theology of the Body*. Cincinnati, OH: Servant, 2005.

Kippley, John F. *Sex and the Marriage Covenant: A Basis for Morality*. Second Edition. San Francisco: Ignatius Press, 2006.

———. *Marriage Is For Keeps: Foundations for Christian Marriage*. Cincinnati, OH: Foundation of the Family, 1994.

Kippley, Sheila. *Breastfeeding and Catholic Motherhood*. Manchester, NH: Sophia Institute Press, 2005.

Lawler, Ronald and others. *Catholic Sexual Ethics: A Summary, Explanation, & Defense*. Second Edition. Huntington, IN: Our Sunday Visitor, 1998.

Lovasik, Lawrence G. *The Catholic Family Handbook*. Manchester, NH: Sophia Institute Press, 2000.

Marks, Frederick. *A Catholic Handbook for Engaged and Newly Married Couples*. Steubenville, OH: Emmaus Road, 2001.

May, William. *Marriage: Rock on Which Family Is Built*. San Francisco: Ignatius Press, 1995.

Mitch, Stacy. *Courageous Love: A Bible Study on Holiness for Women*. Steubenville, OH: Emmaus Road, 1999.

———. *Courageous Virtue: A Bible Study on Moral Excellence for Women*. Steubenville, OH: Emmaus Road, 2000.

———. *Courageous Women: A Study on the Heroines of Biblical History*. Steubenville, OH: Emmaus Road, 2002.

Newland, Mary Reed. *How to Raise Good Catholic Children*. Manchester, NH: Sophia Institute Press, 2004.

Pierlot, Holly. *Mother's Rule of Life: How to Bring Order to Your Home and Peace to Your Soul*. Manchester, NH: Sophia Institute Press, 2004.

Pimentel, Stephen. *Envoy of the Messiah: On Acts of the Apostles 16–28*. Steubenville, OH: Emmaus Road, 2005.

———. *Witnesses of the Messiah: On the Acts of the Apostles 1–15*. Steubenville, OH: Emmaus Road, 2002.

Popcak, Greg. *For Better...Forever!: A Catholic Guide to Lifelong Marriage*. Huntington, IN: Our Sunday Visitor, 2005.

Pope Benedict XVI. Encyclical, On Christian Love *Deus Caritas Est*. December 25, 2005. Available at www.vatican.va.

Pope John Paul II. Apostolic Exhortation On the Role of the Christian Family in the Modern World *Familiaris Consortio*. November 22, 1981. Available at www.vatican.va.

———. Apostolic Letter, On the Dignity and Vocation of Women *Mulieris Dignitatem*. August 15, 1988. Available at www.vatican.va.

———. Encyclical, On The Value and Inviolability of Human Life *Evangelium Vitae*. March 25, 1994. Available at www. vatican.va.

———. *Man and Woman He Created Them: A Theology of the Body*. Translated by Michael M. Waldstein. Boston: Pauline Books & Media, 2006.

Pope Paul VI. Encyclical, On the Regulation of Birth *Humanae Vitae*. July 25, 1968. Available at www.vatican.va.

Pope Pius XI. Encyclical, On Christian Marriage *Casti Connubii*. December 31, 1930. Available at www.vatican.va.

Sarkisian, Rick. *The Mission of the Catholic Family: On the Pathway to Heaven*. San Francisco: Ignatius Press, 2001.

Sheen, Fulton J. *Three To Get Married*. New York: Scepter, 1996 (original copyright 1951).

Smith, Janet. *Why Humanae Vitae Was Right*. San Francisco: Ignatius Press, 1993.

Sri, Edward. *Mystery of the Kingdom*. Steubenville, OH: Emmaus Road, 2000.

Stenson, James. *Anchor: God's Promises of Hope to Parents*. New York: Scepter, 2003.

———. *Compass: A Handbook on Parent Leadership*. New York: Scepter, 2003.

———. *Father, The Family Protector*. New York: Scepter, 2004.

———. *Lifeline: The Religious Upbringing of Your Children*. New York: Scepter, 1997.

———. *Upbringing: A Discussion Handbook for Parents of Young Children*. New York: Scepter, 1992.

Thigpen, Paul. *Building Catholic Family Traditions*. Huntington,

IN: Our Sunday Visitor, 1999.

Van Zeller, Hubert. *Holiness for Housewives: And Other Working Women*. Manchester, NH: Sophia Institute Press, 1997.

Wojtyla, Karol (Pope John Paul II). *Love and Responsibility*. San Francisco: Ignatius Press, 1994.

West, Christopher. *Good News About Sex & Marriage: Honest Questions and Answers about Catholic Teaching*. Cincinnati, OH: Servant, 2004.

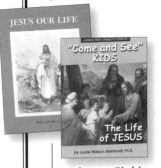

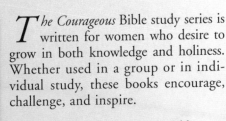